BORN TO SERVE

Power Games in Bureaucracy

Attention Authors

'We Convert Fighters into Writers'. That's the motto of Manas Publications since more than four decades. Our message to the world is that India can win the battle not only by the bullet but also by the pen. There is no dearth of intellectuals in our country, but their knowledge is confined to them only. No sincere effort has been made by any other publisher to channelise their knowledge in national interest. That is why the talent of a large number of intellectuals remains latent. An author transforms his knowledge into a manuscript, and it is our job to spread his/her knowledge by converting it into a beautiful book. For over four decades, Manas has been motivating the intellectuals by publishing their manuscripts and would like to publish your manuscript too. If you or your colleagues have any manuscript ready for publication or are working on it, kindly contact us with detailed synopsis and list of contents. We will transform your work into a valuable publication. If you wish, we can also suggest you the suitable subjects for writing the books related to your area of expertise. Manas is known for its publishing quality and commitments. We take utmost care in production and give wide publicity to the book as well as its author through our national and international distribution network.

BORN TO SERVE

Power Games in Bureaucracy

Dr. Yogendra Narain, IAS (Retd)

Former:

Secretary-General : Rajya Sabha
Defence Secretary : Government of India
Chief Secretary : Uttar Pradesh

Manas Publications

(We Convert Fighters into Writers)

New Delhi - 110 002 (INDIA)

MANAS PUBLICATIONS
(We Convert Fighters into Writers)
(Publishers, Library Suppliers, Importers & Exporters)
4402/5-A, Ansari Road (Opp. HDFC Bank)
Darya Ganj, New Delhi - 110 002 (India)
Phones : Off.: 011-23260783, 23265523, Res.: 011-23842660
E-mail : manaspublications@gmail.com
manaspublications@yahoo.com
Website : www.manaspublications.in

ISBN 978-81-7049-527-7
₹ 795.00

Designed at
Manas Publications

Printed in India at
R.K. Printers, Delhi
and published by Mrs Suman Lata for
Manas Publications, 4402/5-A,
Ansari Road (Opp HDFC Bank),
Darya Ganj, New Delhi - 110 002 (INDIA)

To

my father

LATE SRI KIRPA NARAIN

and my mother

SMT SHANTI DEVI

from whom I imbibed all the cultural
and moral values which stood me in
good stead throughout my life.

IF

If you can keep your head when all about you
Are losing theirs and blaming it on you,
If you can trust yourself when all men doubt you,
But make allowance for their doubting too;
If you can wait and not be tired by waiting,
Or being lied about, don't deal in lies,
Or being hated, don't give way to hating,
And yet don't look too good, nor talk too wise:

If you can dream – and not make dreams your master;
If you can think – and not make thoughts your aim;
If you can meet with Triumph and Disaster
And treat those two impostors just the same;
If you can bear to hear the truth you've spoken
Twisted by knaves to make a trap for fools,
Or watch the things you gave your life to, broken,
And stoop and build 'em up with worn-out tools:

If you can make one heap of all your winnings
And risk it on one turn of pitch-and-toss,
And lose, and start again at your beginnings
And never breathe a word about your loss;
If you can force your heart and nerve and sinew
To serve your turn long after they are gone,
And so hold on when there is nothing in you
Except the Will which says to them: 'Hold on!'

If you can talk with crowds and keep your virtue,
Or walk with Kings – nor lose the common touch,
If neither foes nor loving friends can hurt you,
If all men count with you, but none too much;
If you can fill the unforgiving minute
With sixty seconds' worth of distance run,
Yours is the Earth and everything that's in it,
And – which is more – you'll be a Man, my son!

– Rudyard Kipling

Preface

WRITING an autobiography by a civil servant is not an easy task. Having worked closely as Principal Secretary to three Chief Ministers of UP and also with a Governor during a period of President's Rule, one comes to be closely aware of the goings on beneath the smooth working and sometimes not so smooth working of the government. The cosequential dilemma that arises is, what should be revealed and what not. Certain decisions are taken in confidence and it almost seems a breach of faith to narrate them even now.

When one works in the district, the ripples of such revelations would be confined in most cases to the district and its politicians. As we move up to work in the State secretariats, the effect of lifting the veil of confidentiality would leave its impact on the State level politicians and Ministers, some of whom might be alive and would feel embarrassed. Working in the Centre makes these revelations still more sensitive both to the national level politicians, as well as the nation.

I have tried to seek a balance. I have also narrated many incidents, which might be of interest and learning to those who have joined the service as freshers or who might be suffering the "pangs of outrageous fortune" from the hands of their political masters. In the end I have also given vent to certain unconventional thoughts which have bothered me from time to time. What better place then a book to send ripples in the minds of the captive readers.

The El Dorado that I was seeking was the ideal form of governance for the country. But the Holy Grail eluded me. Perhaps there is no perfect form of governance and what govern the best is the best. As we move along with the Hegelian hypothesis, to every thesis of governance there is an antithesis and every era sees a new synthesis. So the goal post keeps on shifting. Perhaps that is how it should be as human progress cannot stagnate at one level.

I am grateful to my wife Neena with whom I often discuss many issues and get a common sense view of things. My children Deepak, Ashish, and Aparna, together with their spouses Archana, Shilpa and Kartikeya have on many occasions helped me in getting the alternative opinions on many issues. As a civil servant one must learn to mould his views as per the feedback received. My usual strategy used to be to throw an apparently absurd idea and then wait for a strong counter opinion. This disputation would go on till a solution emerged. This was almost like the dialogues of Socrates and Plato. My brother Surendra also provided a sounding board to many of my views on government policies.

From childhood I was deeply inspired by a poem titled "IF" written by Rudyard Kipling. It guided me in all the situations I faced. I feel it necessary to have it included as part of these memoirs as it inspired me throughout my life, both personal and official. Another philosophy that influenced my actions was embedded in the verses of Chapter 12 of the *Bhagavad Gita*. I have included those verses in this book.

I hope the readers will enjoy my experiences as narrated here and also introspect on some of the national issues raised by me.

Dr Yogendra Narain

Contents

CHAPTER 1

Allahabad – The Early Years

I WAS born in 1942 in Meerut, Uttar Pradesh, India. 1942 was the year of Quit India – the year when the Nationalist Movement took the shape of a massive upsurge to oust the British from India. Meerut has a special place in the historic National Movement as it gave birth to the 1857 revolt, later named as the First War of Independence.

My father, late Sri Kirpa Narain Mathur was the Executive Officer of the Meerut Municipal Board. He was a Roorkee trained Civil Engineer and had later served with the Uttar Pradesh Government in the Irrigation Department. I still remember a photograph of him with a solar hat on a horse. He had been trained under the British officers and had great respect for their dedication and devotion to work.

Two years after I was born, there was a vacancy in the Municipal Board at Allahabad, in Uttar Pradesh. He had applied for the same. From the stories that I had heard later, another person, very close to the Congress High Command, had also applied. A directive was issued by the Congress to the local Chairman of the Allahabad Municipal Board, that when the panel of candidates, selected by the Uttar Pradesh Public

Service Commission is considered by the Municipal Committee, the Congress members should vote for the relative of the Congress leader. This was treated by the Congress members of the Municipal Committee, who were in a majority, as a direct interference in the affairs of the local body by the party. They all decided to vote for the candidate listed as number 1 by the Public Service Commission – my father, and ignored the party directive. And thus my father became the Executive Officer of the Allahabad Municipal Board in 1944. The press also took up the matter and there was intense debate on the autonomy of the local bodies. This I learnt through newspaper cuttings of the *Leader*, a respected daily of Allahabad. These cuttings were used as cushions, behind the mirror of a vertical dressing mirror, which my father had brought from a British family returning back to England after the declaration of independence in 1947. My father who was a 'nobody', in Allahabad, suddenly became a 'somebody' in the city which had the privilege of hosting the headquarters of the Congress Party in India located in the Swaraj Bhavan gifted by Motilal Nehru to the Congress. Our entire family moved to Allahabad in 1944 and we stayed there till my father retired in 1964. By that time all my brothers and sisters had got married and I had already appeared for the IAS examination, after topping in my MA in Political Science from Allahabad University.

The twenty years spent in Allahabad were glorious years. I and my siblings had our education in various institutions in Allahabad. I did my Kindergarten and first standard in St Mary's Convent and then moved onto Boys High School in the second standard. Being the youngest in the family I was looked after very well by my sisters and brother and they used to dote over me. One day during an inspection, the District Inspector of Schools, who worked under my father, recognized me immediately. This gave me a new importance.

The nuns in the school were all Irish but there were other teachers too. I acted on the stage for the first time as one of the 'blind men of Hindustan'.

My mother was a staunch activist fighting for the poor and needy ladies. It was my mother who instilled in me not only religious faith and efficacy of prayers, but also the need to help the poor and the needy. She was also a strong nationalist and when she found that my sisters, who were also studying in St Mary's Convent, could not read a letter in Hindi, they were immediately sent to Hindi medium schools.

I remember that during the summer holidays we would go to visit our *Tauji* (father's elder brother) in Delhi. He used to stay in Kinari Bazar, near Chandni Chowk in Old Delhi. On one such trip, when my cousin sister was to get married, we learnt of the sudden assassination of Mahatma Gandhi. My cousin sister was to get married the same day, 30th January 1948. There was no TV in those days but the full commentary of the funeral was broadcast over All India Radio. Every one around me had started crying. I also cried. I realized the value of a popular national leader and also the influence of the Mahatma on the people who looked upon him as a Father, who had led them to Freedom.

On August 15, 1947 a huge public function was held in Allahabad to celebrate India's freedom. A huge wooden platform had been erected in the Exhibition grounds. People had started addressing the mammoth crowd. My brother was also on this platform. Suddenly the platform gave way, as too many people had gathered on the top of it. People fell on one another but nobody got hurt except only my brother – who was as fair as any Englishmen could be. A sharp wooden cleft had cut his nose and he was bleeding. Every one in the crowd was shouting that a handsome boy had been badly hurt. My mother rushed to see him and soon we were in an ambulance going to the hospital. His nose was stitched but a permanent scar, a reminder of the Independence Day of 1947 remained.

In St Mary's Convent they did not allow the boys to continue after the first standard. Apparently the nuns did not trust the boys thereafter. I therefore shifted to the Boys High School but I missed the 'golden toffees' and the 'black toffees' which were sold from a tuck shop in the lunch room, where our tiffins were brought by our servants.

My Boys High School, was a Protestant school, unlike St Mary's Convent which was Catholic. I learnt to understand Christianity, in the midst of being brought up by my Hindu parents, who were deeply religious. I remember taking my mother early in the winter mornings for the 'Kartik Snan' (bath) in the 'Sangam'. There was food and money to be given to the poor, who would line up on the route from the car to the 'Sangam'. Many fasts were observed and my mother and elder sister gave up eating meat. There were numerous servants in the house, but all were treated with respect. My parents taught me to respect the poor and the weak.

In 1954 there was a big Kumbh Mela in Allahabad. This festival comes once in twelve years in the city and the Hindus come to have a bath at the Sangam in Allahabad. The Sangam is a confluence of three rivers, namely the Ganga, the Yamuna and the invisible Saraswati. Since my father was the Executive Officer of the Allahabad Municipal Board, and was responsible for all the municipal services in the Kumbh Mela area, we had our own spacious tent, which had everything like a kitchen, toilets, bathing spaces, sleeping places etc, in the Kumbh Mela area on the banks of the Sangam.

On the main bathing day our family proceeded on foot towards the Sangam. We had our servants with us carrying our clothes and food. As we were proceeding, suddenly we saw the Nagas, on elephants on the same route. The Nagas are people who are normally naked and they move in groups called Akharas. The time of bathing of each Akhara is fixed by the district administration. They are ferocious people who can get angry very soon and are feared even by the authorities. Suddenly there was a stampede as one of the elephants ran amok. People started running and some fell down. People ran over them. My mother sensed that there was something wrong and told my father to go back. We swiftly moved back to our tent.

Next day we learnt that more than forty people had died in that very area, where we were. What added to the situation going out of control, was the fact that the police which was meant to control the Naga procession had been redeployed for VIP duty as the Prime Minister was expected. We thanked God for our lucky escape.

In school, I was chosen to participate in elocution contests as well as plays. Gilbert Bose, who was our Maths teacher, trained me and my friend Romesh Gulati in the art of debating. In our first venture, outside school, we participated in an Inter-School debating competition and won the shield. It was a big day for us. This stood me in good stead in later life when I was to address huge gatherings as a public servant. I represented the school in all the games, as I consciously wanted to be an all-rounder. I was a reasonably good hockey and football player, a dark horse in cricket, and a sincere athlete. Once I decided to participate in a marathon race, as a member of my House team (Blue House), simply because very few of our house boys were participating. Our Blue House participants got very low positions but in totality the House stood first. Through games I learnt the values of camaraderie and team work. I feel very proud to mention that the famous actor Amitabh Bachchan was our contemporary in school. He was a student of Boys High School till the seventh standard, after which he moved over to Sherwood College, Nainital. He was one year senior to me but we did act in small skits or plays together. As was the practice at that time, the immediate junior class boys would buy books from the immediate senior class boys at half the price. I remember one year I went to his house to buy some secondhand books from him. After hard negotiations (he wanted a higher price for some well-kept books) we settled and I paid him in Rupees, *annas* and pies. In school, he was accepted as a good actor on stage. One year he won the Best Actor Award, and in another year (1958), I did. I also won the Tresham Medal for being the Best Boy in school.

As I wanted to be an all-rounder, I also decided to learn swimming and tennis. The Bharadwaj swimming tank in Allahabad was ideal for learning swimming. The teacher made us cross the river Yamuna in one month. I took Tennis coaching in the Gymkhana. I was inspired to learn tennis as my close friend and classfellow Pradeep Bhargava, was the State tennis champion, both in tennis and table tennis. But I found it difficult to continue with all the sports, as my house was at a distance, and I had to cycle all the way. Eventually Badminton became my first love as I had a Badminton court next to my house in the Municipal Board compound.

After doing my Senior Cambridge in 1958, I joined the Ewing Christian College, in Allahabad for doing my

Intermediate. It was while in College that I became fond of numerology and astrology which was influenced by my uncle, Mukat Behari, who was a well-known astrologer in our family. I still have his records. I later read Cheiro's palmistry on my own and was able, in later years, to exactly predict the marriage of my IAS colleague, Sumita Kandpal, while she was posted in Lucknow.

I carried forward with gusto my love for debates and dramatics in the Ewing Christian College as well as the University. Here I came in contact with Professor Rajamani of the English Department of the Allahabad University. He had seen me debating in the inter college debating contests and picked me up as soon as I joined the University. I became a member of the debating team of the Allahabad University in all the inter-University competitions. I won several Gold medals in the debates organized by the Allahabad University Students Union as well as in the inter-Hostel debates. I was selected to participate in plays and was quite active on the stage. I was invited to be a member of the Muir Hostel, the most prestigious Hostel of the University. I then began representing the Muir Hostel in debates.

This Hostel had developed another tradition with the inmates of the Women's Hostel. The girls would give titles on Holi to selected boys of the Muir Hostel. I still remember the title I got. It was a lyric of a film song which ran as *"Mai Kamsin Hu, Nadan Hu"*.

The naughtiest thing I ever did in Allahabad University was to climb the Muir Tower in the Science Faculty. The idea was born out of pure mischief merely because we were barred from climbing it. I remember Vinod Vaish, Ashok (Tillu) and two or three others who were partners in this mischief. It would have gone off well except that Ashok started aiming his torchlight at a function in the open area below. Unfortunately the University Proctor was also in the function. He sent the University guards to catch us.

When the guards came at the bottom of the Tower they asked us to come down. We kept quiet. The guards did not have the courage to climb the Tower in the dark night. After some time they went off. We waited an hour and then came down quietly.

There was another very prestigious club in the Allahabad University called the Friday Club. It was basically a Club of the English Department but some people from other departments were also inducted. I was inducted on the same day as Mrinal Pandey, who later became the Editor of *Hindustan*. She was the daughter of the famous poetess Shivani. It included Professors of the English Department as well as selected students. The Club had a tradition of papers being read by the members on any subject of their choice and this was followed by intensive discussions. I remember I read a paper on "Is Science a Superstition?" I thoroughly enjoyed being a member of this Club.

Another Club of which I was fortunate to become a member was the Elysium Club. We used to meet in the Barnett's Hotel. We had outstanding speakers to address us. It was guided in its activities by one of the founding members Veeri Datta. It provided a great opportunity for intellectual discussions and also gave us an opportunity to present our own papers. Membership was very restricted. My brother Surendra Narain Mathur later took the initiative in establishing and activising the Elysium Club in Delhi. We follow the precedents set up in Allahabad.

As a result though I did well in both, debates and dramatics (including representing Allahabad University at the

National Youth Festival in 1961). I did not do well in the BSc examination which required concentration. I thereafter switched over to Political Science for my Masters degree and surprisingly topped in the Class. This gave me a coveted medal in the Convocation. Another medal, the Seshadiri Gold Medal was also awarded to me for writing the Best Essay in English in the University. Being a topper also got me a job as a lecturer in the Political Science Department on a leave vacancy for five months. That was my first job and my mother was thrilled when I gave her my first salary of ₹ 300. I still remember that when I went to take my first class of MA Previous students, my Head of Department AB Lal, insisted on escorting me and introducing me to the students. He was afraid that they may think that I may be another student as I looked very young!

Political Science let me understand the political thought of Aristotle, Socrates, Plato, St Augustus, Machiavelli, Rousseau, Locke, and so on. Public Administration was also a part of the course. I thoroughly relished political philosophy and was inspired by these great thinkers.

In Allahabad, I closely witnessed the political life of the city. Bishambhar Nath Pande, a historian and an active Congressman, was the Chairman of the Allahabad Municipal Board, where my father was the Executive Officer. A gracious man, with a flowing beard, he often came to our house. He later became the Governor of Orissa. Lal Bahadur Shastri, was another frequent visitor to our house. I remember that when he got elevated to become the Minister of Railways, he requested my father to join him in Delhi. However, on our request, my father preferred to stay on in Allahabad. Later on, I had the privilege of serving under his son, Sunil Shastri, when I was the Secretary, Power in Uttar Pradesh and he was the Minister of Power.

Sri HN Bahuguna, was another frequent visitor to our house. Bahuguna was then a respected and powerful Congressman of Allahabad. He later became the Chief Minister of Uttar Pradesh. I was always a recipient of his love and affection, because of my father. By a strange follow-up in history, when I was Chief Secretary, Uttar Pradesh in 1998, his daughter Rita Bahuguna, was the Mayor of Allahabad.

My father was the senior most Executive Officer amongst the Municipal Officers of Uttar Pradesh in the late fifties. Because of his excellent record, he was offered the newly created post of Administrator of the Gorakhpur Municipal Corporation. However, all of us pressed him to stay on in Allahabad because of our studies. Bowing to our wishes, my father declined the offer. The post of Administrator was then made a cadre post for the IAS.

In the '50s we still had the ICS officers. My parents used to tell me about their participation in the Commissioner's parties. They wanted their sons to be a part of the grandeur of officialdom. We were inspired to sit for the All India Service examinations and rise to be District Magistrates, Commissioners and Governor. The grounds had been laid in the classroom of the Faculty of Political Science. The seed was sown in our minds. I appeared for the All India Service Examinations along with more than two lakh aspirants from all over India. With God's blessing and the prayers of my parents I secured tenth rank in the Indian Administrative Service (IAS) and ninth in the Indian Foreign Service (IFS). That year there were three people who got in the first ten positions from Allahabad – Rajani Kant Verma, Mainak Bose and myself. My mother asked me to opt for the IAS and I did so. In 1965 I got my appointment. In the subsequent examination in the, Lal Bahadur Shastri National Academy of

Administration, I rose to the third position in the all India ranking, and started my training as a Sub-Divisional Magistrate in Aligarh.

Coming from middle class families into the IAS has a distinct advantage. To care for the poor and have sympathy for them becomes ingrained in us. One has to fight and establish himself at every point in the career by hard work, dedication and loyalty to the organization. There is no one to support you, unlike those who are second and third generation civil servants. You have to earn respect and your only USP is your sincerity and honesty. You have to tread carefully because as administrators, rule and regulations bind you while your heart stretches out to do something different. You have to be well versed not only in man management but also in knowing how to handle your bureaucrat bosses as well as your political bosses. The higher you rise, the more you get involved in policy-making. You pick up the art of moving forward without compromise. At this point you start experimenting in administration. There are no readymade solutions to every problem you face because problems change their contours. Senior people can only share their experiences. It is for the juniors to learn the principles and see how to apply them. Administration then becomes a sharing of experiments, in which sometimes you win, sometimes fail.

Chapter 2

Lal Bahadur Shastri National Academy of Administration

AFTER reporting to the Director of the Lal Bahadur Shastri National Academy of Administration in July 1965 we had a combined Foundation Course of studies for four months with all those who had qualified in the Civil Services – the Indian Administrative Service, the Indian Foreign Service and other Central Services. The friendships generated, stood us in great stead throughout our service and we could network through these nascent friendships to sort out various problems we would face from time to time in our administrative careers later on. We learnt to respect each other, irrespective of the service we were in.

I experimented here for the first time in the Academy, the art of contesting elections. I stood for the post of Secretary, Fine Arts Society. I felt shy in approaching each probationer with a request to vote for me. I learnt however, from this experiment that each person is important because each person has one vote. I learnt from this experience that your esteem and strength does not depend on the service you belong to but your merit and qualification. I won the election.

Even after winning the elections it is necessary to prove that you are the right choice and the voters had justifiably put their trust in you. One has to take the initiative and learn to be a leader because the voter is very demanding. I organized several programmes even though it required a lot of coaxing to persuade people to participate.

In organizing the programmes, I learnt a bitter lesson which left a deep impression within me. I had organized a play in Hindi called 'Inspector'. It was a Three-Act play and since it was long, I did not mix any other programme with it. However, two days before the programme I was summoned to the office of the Joint Director to answer a complaint lodged by one of the probationers. This probationer had complained that I was anti-South as in the cultural programme I had not included any South Indian item. I told the Joint Director that it was a Three-Act play which I had organized and that is why I had not included any other variety item, eg dance and music either from the North or the South. But the complainant was persistent and the Joint Director asked me to include a South Indian dance programme as a compromise. We worked out the logistics. Since the opening scene of the play had a pre-set arrangement of tables and furniture and could not be dismantled it was decided to have the dance outside the stage. A boundary of flower pots was arranged and the South Indian dance was held within it on the floor in front of the stage.

This was the first time I came in contact with this feeling of being North Indian or South Indian. In the schools, college and University I studied, I had never experienced this feeling. We were always all one, all Indians. But I learnt that in the wider world even though the number of persons who held this divisive view were very few, but yet they existed. In administration one has to always keep this at the back of one's mind.

The Bharat Darshan tour which we undertake as probationers gives us a wide experience of the country and her people. It is very educative and informative. It made us to appreciate those freedom fighters who not only fought for our independence but brought us together. I understood why Mahatma Gandhi had first chosen to travel by train throughout the length and breadth of the country, before he took over the leadership of the independence movement. During this tour we also met the Prime Minister, Sri Lal Bahadur Shastri, and were impressed with his simplicity.

Later, after a couple of months, we also had to serve out our attachment with the Army. We learnt first-hand knowledge about the hard lives the defence officers have to live on our borders. One scene which I can never forget is our stay in the dug out (bunker) where, though an opening, a gun was constantly aimed at the bunker of the enemy on the other side. Besides the gun, was a hard wooden bed where the soldiers sit and sleep with buzzing mosquitoes all round. I was sure that a similar set-up was there on the Pakistani side as well. Between the two there was empty barren land where nobody went and nobody could cultivate. While admiring our brave soldiers, it left me wondering over the senseless violence we engage in for a border which exists only in latitudes and longitudes – my territory and your territory. We die protecting the imaginary line. Who is to be blamed?

It made me realize that many things happen in life which are irrational yet they are rational for those who had been personally affected, in the present case those whose relatives had been killed during the migration that followed the Partition. For those who had seen their brothers, sisters and parents killed before their eyes, Partition was real. The division of territories was real. For those who had suffered and lived there would be no compromise, at least not in their lifetime. Later generations might obliterate the division based on religion, but that would take time. Till then we will continue to fight and defend; to threaten and bleed each other. History of course teaches that time is a greater healer. France, Germany, the UK and the USA have learnt to live with each other after the Second World War. Japan, on whom the US used the Atom Bomb had become a 'Natural ally' of the western world. As a student of Political Science and European History I wondered when this change would come in our subcontinent. Consciously it would come late, but unconsciously it might come earlier.

With these thoughts, one came back to the Academy. It left me disturbed. It made me realize that life is both rational and irrational. It made me realize that national policies can be made in the heat of the moment but cannot be unmade when the environment cools down. Our men are getting killed on the borders and are killing those on the opposite side. Each of such brave men are getting medals and commendations for these very acts. And yet we say we are at the acme of civilization. We have overthrown and eliminated the barbarians who lived in the past and had no laws. The most powerful ruled and exploited the lesser ones. But are we not doing the same today? Only the methods have changed. Thinking has not.

After the army attachment we went through our final examination in the Academy. This also included a test for horse riding. We had to do the high jump with our horse as well as canter, trot and gallop. While galloping my female horse suddenly took off. My legs got out of the stirrups and I was thrown on the neck of the horse. I however kept my cool. While my instructor Nawal Singh, watched with bated breath (he was sure I would be thrown off). I folded my arms around the neck of the horse. Slowly I put my left leg in the stirrup to be followed by the right leg in the right stirrup. Then I got back on the saddle and slowly pulled the reins. The horse gradually came under control and I took it with a slow trot back to the instructor. Nawal Singh, my instructor was extremely pleased with my presence of mind and coolness. I, of course, passed the horse riding test successfully.

This incident revealed to me my own nature. I could be patient and cool. I was not frustrated. I felt confident. In my future life, this incident would remain as a lesson to be remembered. Anything could have happened to me if I had been nervous or dependent on somebody else to save me. One must learn to survive on one's own.

The results of the examination of the Academy improved my position further from being tenth in the All India examination to be the third in the IAS. I was quite excited. I also got the Cadre of my choice, ie Uttar Pradesh – my own home state. My parents were equally delighted. Their son was now going to be equivalent to the ICS – he would go up to be a District Magistrate, a Commissioner and later on, if God was kind, even a Governor. In childhood, my mother used to sing a lullaby.

Hey Baby, *ho balwan*
Duniya may kar apna nam
Gandhi *jaise veer banna*
Nehru *jaise insaan*
He baby, *ho balwan*.

In the British days, the ICS were considered a part of the heaven born. Nehru and Gandhi were the political icons. Everyone wanted their children to be moulded on the pattern of Mahatma Gandhi and Nehru. However, in government service even in the fifties, the IAS, which was patterned on the ICS, was the foremost choice. Though the ICS was the steel frame of the British and hated by the Indians, yet, since the steel frame continued intact after independence (renamed as IAS) everyone wanted their children in the IAS. It carried power and prestige. Service to the country was a second thought. Moreover, in most of the North Indian States, where industrialization was yet to come, government service for the middle classes, was the preferred choice.

My father, late Sri Kirpa Narain, was the Chief Executive Officer of the Allahabad Municipal Board for almost twenty years. Everybody knew about him. He was popular because of his integrity and hard work. I used to see many political figures like Lal Bahadur Shastri, Hemvati Nandan Bahuguna, Bishambhar Nath Pande, Chunan Guru, Satya Prakash Malviya, etc, in our house. Twenty-four hours water supply was introduced in Allahabad in my father's time. My parents often used to be invited for parties at the house of the Commissioner and that is where they were inspired to see their sons in government service, especially in the IAS. And that is how I landed in the Academy for training.

As the training ended, I got my orders from the Government of Uttar Pradesh appointing me as Assistant Magistrate, Aligarh. My father had in the meantime shifted to Agra after his retirement. Aligarh being close to Agra, I could see my parents every weekend. I used to travel by bus. Often it was very embarrassing as at times my co-passenger would be the person I was trying in my court.

Chapter 3

My First Innings in Uttar Pradesh – Aligarh, Mirzapur, Kanpur and Lucknow

WHEN I reported for duty at Aligarh, I was summoned before the District Magistrate. His name was NS Sirohi. A burly, hefty figure in his fifties, he was sitting, wearing a *Baniyan* (vest) in his office. It was extremely hot. I had expected to see a well-dressed man wearing a tie – the prototype of the British ICS District Magistrate in my mind. He welcomed me while munching his *'paan supari'*. After some initial enquiries, he summoned both his ADMs (Additional District Magistrates), Girish Chandra and Sharma, and introduced me to them. I was introduced as the *'Junt Sahib'* meaning the Joint Magistrate. After putting all of us at ease, he asked all of us our qualifications. We were all either MAs or BA LLBs. Then he gave a loud guffaw and said in chaste Hindi – *"Tum sub Chutiya ho"* (a Hindi abuse). I was shocked I had never spoken such an abuse, and did not expect a District Magistrate to say this. Observing the studied silence on our faces, he laughed again and said – "I have only studied up to Intermediate (Class XII) and I am your boss. Is this not funny?" We all joined in his laughter – there was no other option.

NS Sirohi had risen from being a Tehsildar to District Magistrate. The British used to directly recruit people from respected and loyal families to junior posts in the government. They would rise according to their hard work and merit. Sirohi was known as a tough administrator. He was a Jat and had been sent to Aligarh to control the communal riots in the city which had erupted a month back. He had successfully brought the situation under control.

There were no jeeps given to the officers at that time, except to the District Magistrate. We used to go to our sub-divisions by bus, boats and elephant/horses. Sometimes if we were lucky we could hitch a ride with the ADM (Planning) who had recently been given a Jeep by the government like all other ADMs (Planning) in Uttar Pradesh. There was no TV and the news came to us through the radio and newspapers. Orders from the government came through teleprinters and later by FAX. There were no computers and no calculators. Life was simple though not easy going.

At the time of the General Elections we got vehicles as Assistant Returning Officers and Magistrates. We were required to check the location of the polling booths. On the day prior to the polling we were to ensure that all the polling parties had reached with ballot boxes. The election system in India is running successfully since the last sixty years. Every officer who is involved in the conduct of the election does his duty with dedication and devotion. Even during our training, election duty is the most important component. Reaching inaccessible villages by foot, ensuring that nobody is prevented from voting, ensuring that anti-social elements or the local *goondas* do not forcibly promote voting for a particular candidate is our *dharma*. We are tested accordingly by our seniors.

Trying cases as a Sub-District Magistrate is equally interesting. Human society is full of man created problems. Whether it be revenue cases or criminal cases we are committed to giving justice according to the law. Whether the law itself is just or unjust is not judged at junior levels. The law as it stands, is our only guide at the junior level of magistracy.

During my training in Aligarh, I was given charge of Sub-Divisional Magistrate of Atrauli. As mentioned, earlier we had no jeeps and we used to travel to the villages by bus and from the last bus stop, journey by foot or bullock cart or horse and once on an elephant. The infrastructure in the rural areas was very poor. Metalled roads were a rarity. The one journey I did on the elephant was because there was no way to cross the river to go to the village where I had to do *partal*. *'Partal'* meant verifying the ownership and boundaries of every field, ensuring correctness of the entries in the *Khasra* (field verification of crops, wells and trees on a particular plot) and *Khatauni* (record of ownership of land). I was accompanied by the Tehsildar (Tehsil Revenue Chief)), Naib Tehsildar (his deputy) and the Lekhpal (in-charge of the village records). All the villagers would gather at one spot and would confirm if the entries were correct. An SDM is an important official and normally there would be either one or two tehsils under him. The SDM would be trying both revenue and criminal cases in his jurisdiction as there was no separation of judiciary from the executive. The separation came by an amendment to the Criminal Procedure Code in 1973. Only an SDM could issue orders under Section 144 of the CrPC, banning procession or banning the assembling of more than four people. He was allowed to attach disputed property if there was apprehension of breach of peace, pending final decision of the court. The

SDM was allowed to detain person under Section 110 CrPC if anyone was found loitering in suspicious circumstances. Thus, the SDM was looked upon with respect by both the Police and the revenue machinery, and as a *mai-baap* by the people to settle disputes and give relief at the time of distress, eg droughts and floods.

At the village level the order of SDM were treated as sacrosanct. Once I remember I was on winter tour and it had got very late. I reached a village late at night and asked if there was any dispute in the village. Two groups came forward and said they had a dispute over a piece of land and this dispute has been in the court for the last twenty years. I asked them whether they would respect my decision. After they said "yes", I gave them a patient hearing. The time was 10 o'clock in the night and my tehsildar was nudging me to leave. I got up and asked for a rope. Then I went to the disputed piece of land and had the rope stretched out diagonally, dividing the plot half and half. I then announced imperiously that the portion on the left would now belong to 'A' and the other half to the party 'B'. There were protests but the whole village persuaded the two parties to accept the decision of the SDM, ie me. After this I came back to the district headquarters. I heard later that the lawyers of both the parties persuaded their clients to appeal in court against the decision. The final appeal was heard in the Supreme Court which upheld my decision and said that as the SDM had decided the dispute on the spot therefore they will not interfere in the matter.

It was while I was posted as SDM Atrauli that I first met Kalyan Singh who later became the Chief Minister of Uttar Pradesh. He was a young, bright upcoming politician and had come to see me in connection with an election matter relating to the Municipal Board of Atrauli.

During this period I was called on emergency duty twice. First it was in Lucknow, when there was a strike in the Secretariat. Jagdish Khattar and I were made Staff Officers to the then Chief Secretary KK Das, ICS. I was put in-charge of fresh recruitment of officials in place of those dismissed from service. Some of those recruited were still working when I retired. The second call for emergency duty was in the drought-stricken district of Mirzapur. SAT Rizvi, Jagdish Khattar and I were posted for relief work. It was here that I met for the first time, Karnail Singh of the 1964 batch. We were to share the same house. After the transfer of the District Magistrate (RN Azad), RK Bhargava joined as the District Magistrate. He was an energetic officer, very active and a field officer in the real sense. He and his wife were very affectionate and I was often called for meals at his house.

In Mirzapur there was a troublesome politician called Gramwasi. Soon after the drought, heavy rains followed and flooding started in the district. Sri Bhargava wanted to tour the flood affected areas in a boat. Gramwasi insisted that he would also come. He kept on criticizing the district administration throughout. Soon RK Bhargava stopped the boat and all of us got down at a village. Within five minutes RK Bhargava promptly got on the boat with all the officers and left Gramwasi behind. Sri Gramwasi kept on shouting to wait for him as the village was surrounded by water. But Sri Bhargava asked him to stay back and organize the relief work.

We had a PCS Officer by the name AK Jain who was in-charge of distribution of relief material. Once when I went to see him at his residence, I found a large portion of files on the left side and an equal number of files on his right side. I asked him the reason. He said in total confidence, "There is a lot of relief material coming in the district. I am sure there will be an enquiry afterward. So, I am having duplicate files prepared, to enable me to answer the queries later on." I was amused. Obviously Sri Jain had suffered from enquiries earlier.

I got married to Neena in 1967. We were shown each other in Agra at the Taj Mahal. I went to Raebareli for the marriage. My father-in-law was the Superintendent of Police. I had seen Neena for the first time in a photograph in the newspaper when she had topped in Uttar Pradesh in the Intermediate exams.

In 1968, I was appointed City Magistrate of Kanpur. I knew my predecessor NC Saxena and his wife Naomi from Allahabad. My wife Neena also knew both of them. The City Magistrate's bungalow was a very spacious one with a drive. When I learnt from NC Saxena that there was a daily allowance of ₹ 80 for the City Magistrate if he possessed a car, I acquired my first car from Deshraj Singh and Lata Singh, the previous owners of the Fiat Millecento. My wife Neena and I felt very proud to own this car.

The peon of the City Magistrate was a tall hefty fellow. He was polished in his manners as well as in the art of getting tips. Once we went to see a film in a cinema hall. He promptly informed the hall owner who came to receive my wife and myself at the entrance. A big crowd had gathered, my peon made way by walking in front and making way for us. After walking some distance, he noticed that I was struggling at the back. He promptly rescued me.

Once an interesting case came before me in the court. A girl had eloped with her boyfriend and got married. Her father had lodged a complaint in the local police station and the case came before me after she had been recovered. In her statement before me she stated that she had gone willingly with the boy.

But the father insisted that she had been kidnapped and should be in his custody pending final decision. The boy opposed this request saying that she was his wife and should remain with him. The public prosecutor mischievously stated that pending final decision she should stay with the court. I thought, "Stay with the court" meant staying with me and got horrified. I said, "No, No." The Public Prosecutor noting the concern in my voice clarified that by staying with the court meant being in court custody in the local Nari Niketan. I promptly passed the order. I also noticed that both the groups had brought a large number of people with them and there was tension in the air. I then adjourned the case for hearing for two days. On the second day I told the prosecutor to bring the girl promptly at 10 o'clock which was the official time of the court opening. At 10 AM sharp I recorded the girl's statement and the certificate showing her as a major. I allowed her to go with the boy. At 11 AM the parents came and protested but the order had already been passed. The tension got defused.

The next year I got transferred as Deputy Secretary, Department of Finance, Government of Uttar Pradesh. Accommodation was a severe problem. However, the late Varadarajan, who was then the Secretary to the Uttar Pradesh State Electricity Board, got me a place to stay in one of the guest houses of the Board. My Finance Secretary was Sri Bharat Ram, who had been in finance for umpteen years. Amongst the many departments, which I had to handle, from the Finance side was the Uttar Pradesh Sugar Corporation. A proposal had come from the Sugar Corporation for a government guarantee for a loan being raised by the Corporation. The proposal was examined at the lower level and recommended for rejection. Arvind Verma who was the Joint Secretary looking after the Corporation, came to me and explained why the guarantee was necessary. I found the proposal justified and overriding the objections raised by the 'stalwarts' of the Finance Department, I recommended the proposal for approval of the Finance Secretary. The file came back promptly next day, duly approved. I was very happy and so was Arvind. But the happiness was short lived. The next day I was summoned with the file to the Finance Secretary's room. He was very annoyed and asked the reason why I had overridden the objection raised. I put forward the arguments which Arvind had told me. Sri Bharat Ram was extremely annoyed and ordered the file to be sent to him once again. He reversed his orders and cancelled the guarantee. I learnt my lesson. In Finance Department, the file pushing seasoned babus are the ones whose wisdom should be respected. They are the one who 'know'.

Narayan Dutt Tiwari was my Finance Minister. Once, an officer, who was looking after the Uttar Pradesh State Lotteries, proceeded on long leave, and I was appointed as Director of the Uttar Pradesh State Lotteries. In the first lottery that I conducted, I showed a profit. In the meantime, the regular Director, Lotteries came back. I was about to give him back his charge, when orders came from the Finance Minister that I was to be the regular Director, Lotteries and the other officer was given an insignificant charge. I later learnt that Narayan Dutt Tiwari was very pleased as I had turned a loss-making lottery into a profitable one. That was my first contact with Narayan Dutt Tiwari. He was development-oriented and chose his officers with care.

As Director Lotteries, I travelled extensively. I met the lottery agents, took their suggestions, and acted upon them. We had a continuous run of profits. I then learnt a lesson, which had stood me well in my administrative career. The best suggestions in any field come from those who are a part of it, not from those outside.

My first air travel came when I decided to go to Patna, to meet the Director, State Lotteries, Bihar. After the sad demise of Bharat Narain, we got a very liberal Finance Secretary SVS Juneja, who encouraged me in any new initiative I took. While boarding the plane for the first time, I found that unlike my car tyres, plane tyres were a bit flat! Overcoming all inhibitions, (life is precious), I went up to where the ground staff was standing, and pointed to the tyres. They smiled and asked me not to worry!

I saw another characteristic of Narayan Dutt Tiwari. He could never say no, to anybody and secondly he would meet everyone, who came to see him. Once, I literally saw him, leave one visitor in the main hall, move over to the sitting room to talk confidentially to another visitor, leave him there and then meet a third person near the toilet, and then after finishing talking to him, come back to the main hall once again. He would not annoy anybody.

Narayan Dutt Tiwari also made intensive studies of the topics he was going to speak about in the legislature. He would go to the Library, make extensive notes, and then speak in the House. I learnt a lot from him.

The Chief Secretary, BB Lal, called me one day to his office. He said that I was being posted as District Magistrate, Muzaffarnagar and wished me best of luck. In his usual style, he guffawed, and advised me to work hard. In those days all postings were done by Chotte Lal and Bade Lal. Chotte Lal was the Under Secretary in the Appointments Department while Bade Lal was of course BB Lal, ICS!

This was going to be my first district charge and I was very excited.

As soon as I landed in Muzaffarnagar, I received a letter from Virendra Verma, a very prominent politician and a former minister under Chaudhary Charan Singh, a Jat leader and former Chief Minister of Uttar Pradesh. In his handwritten note, he advised me that in order to be successful in Muzaffarnagar, I must concentrate more on the villages and rural areas, as this district was predominantly an agricultural area. I took his advice to heart.

In the western districts of Uttar Pradesh, the dominant community was the Jat community. They are basically of a loving nature, very affectionate, but with a rough exterior. In Allahabad, where I was brought up, when we address a person, we call him *'Aap'*. But here I was shocked to be addressed as *'Tu'* which we, in Allahabad, addressed to someone younger. I later learnt that the persons they love and respect are addressed as *'Tu'* by the Jats.

I extensively toured the rural areas. Their basic demands were fertilizer, seeds and water. They did not require any other help from the administration. Land was extremely valuable to them and this I learnt, when I visited the District Jail for the first time. There were at least thirty women, who were incarcerated in jail for either killing their husbands or their sons or near relatives, only for the sake of getting land in their name.

In 1975 there was a scarcity of foodgrains. Wheat was selling at ₹3 per kilo which was almost the double the price as it was selling two months earlier. The poor were unable to buy wheat, which was their staple diet.

I convened a meeting of the foodgrain wholesalers and retailers and requested them to help in selling wheat to individuals at ₹2 per kilo, with a maximum quantity of twenty kilos per family. I told the wholesalers that it would go a long way in building their credit and would alleviate the misery of the poor and middle-class. They readily agreed and we promptly set up several sale points in the city under this scheme. The scheme was highly popular and brought immense goodwill to the administration as well as the wheat traders. The poor were greatly benefited.

Emergency was imposed in the country in the intervening night of the 25th and 26th June 1975. We enjoyed immense powers. But the ruling party MLAs, MPs and their stooges wanted the powers to be exercised as per their wishes. They wanted their political opponents to be detained and put under MISA (Maintenance of Internal Security Act). Names of those to be detained came from the State Government to the police, who then took the advice of the Public Prosecutor in framing the charge sheet whereupon the proposal was put up to the District Magistrate for approval. The District Magistrate was expected to scrutinize the documents, "apply his mind" and sign the detention order.

Any critical comments of the government in any newspaper would lead to the detention and arrest of the journalist and/or the editor.

The ruling party members took it upon themselves to portray the Emergency as a blessing. It is however also true, that during the Emergency, the Railways were running on time, officers were in their offices punctually on time, respect for the police and administration increased, orders of the administration were complied with and discipline was prevailing in society.

In Muzaffarnagar, many of the suggestions of the ruling party came as orders. But in one case, I had to take a stand. There was a particular issue of the price at which tea should be sold by the vendors plying their *thelas*. The ruling party bigwigs wanted the tea to be sold at ₹ 1 per cup instead of ₹ 3 per cup. They approached me to ensure compliance as it would make the Emergency popular, amongst the masses. I talked to the vendors who were basically small time shopkeepers. They said that the sugar prices were very high and if sugar prices could be reduced they could sell tea at lower prices. When I went back to the leaders of the ruling party, amongst whom were some sugar commission agents (the leader being a member of the ruling party), they said, that the sugar prices were governed by the market and they could not lower the sugar prices. I then told them plainly, not to pursue the idea of selling tea at one rupee. The matter ended.

Khatauli is a subdivision of Muzaffarnagar. There was a bone crushing factory, which used to emit an obnoxious smell when working. We had tried to ban the factory under Section 144 of the CrPC but the factory owner had refused to comply with the order. The residents, living nearby, were complaining again and again as it affected their health.

The Emergency gave the administration a good opportunity. We issue a MISA detention order against him and pasted it on the premises of the factory. The factory closed soon thereafter and the owner absconded. He did not come back as long as the Emergency lasted and the residents heaved a sigh of relief.

Once based on the information given by the police, I had issued a detention order under MISA, against a former MLA of the opposition. He absconded. Some days later, I received a message that his wife was seriously ill and that he wanted to see her. He requested that he may not be arrested during the period he spent in the house with his wife. I talked to the Superintendent of Police and advised him to let the ex-MLA visit his wife and not to arrest him. The SP agreed as it appeared a humanitarian cause. The ex-MLA remained ever grateful to me for this gesture. It was a lesson for me that power should always be used in a humane manner.

Emergency showed me that the fear or threat of action is always greater than the action itself. During this period, because of fear of arrest, everybody acted in a disciplined manner. The planes flew on schedule, there were no strikes, trains were extremely punctual, and police was ready to act firmly. Corruption also went down. Of course, it also led to misuse of authority. There was a strict control over the press. Though there was no press censorship in the district but immediate arrests were made, if any article was written against the government. Thc press would be sealed and the journalist detained. Nobody would have the courage to go to court. Crime also went down. Most of the criminals were detained under MISA.

There was an owner of a tractor agency who had taken advances but had not supplied the tractors. MISA detention orders were issued against him. Tractors were promptly supplied.

Jayaprakash, the famous opposition leader, came to address the citizens of Muzaffarnagar. A very large crowd came to see him. Both the SP and I were also keen to meet him and we sat through the entire speech. Later I learnt that the local Congressmen complained to the government that we were sympathetic to JP. However, nothing happened. But this was the atmosphere of suspicion prevailing at that time.

The workers of the ruling party kept a tight vigil on prices as well as the press and the action of the opposition leaders. The instructions given to them were to show the Emergency in a good light and to show how it was good for the country.

In retrospect I think Emergency was good for the country but not good for the people. Hundreds of people were put behind bars merely for the reason that they were opposed to the promulgation of the Emergency. The government officials at the lower levels got more power to harass people, if they wanted to. Any resistance to authority, including its misuse, would be treated as sedition and arrest would be imminent.

Furthermore, the powers given to the government officials during Emergency were used to forcibly push well-intentioned programmes like Family Planning. Persuasion strategy of the pre-Emergency period gave way to coercion during the Emergency period. Muslims were the worst victims of this strategy. In Muzaffarnagar after I had left the district, it led to firing by the police leading to deaths of more than two dozen people, young and old. Family planning success was viewed statistically. How many cases has one brought for sterilization? This was the criteria on which one's performance was judged.

However, it set me thinking. Why was it that during the Emergency the entire government machinery was moving in a disciplined manner? Was everybody afraid of the stick? Is that the way that the government should run to get the best results? Even the *Ramayana* says that you must keep under strict check, the people of the lower castes, women and animals if 'people of the lower castes' can be metamorphosed to mean 'government servants' and 'women' can be meant to mean the 'middle men, power brokers and animals'. To mean 'criminals and traitors' then all that it means is that government can only work if it keeps a tight leash on all of them.

During my stay in Muzaffarnagar I was informed about a criminal tribe settled in Muzaffarnagar called the Bawariyas. The British had settled them in a contiguous area near Oon

Block of Shamli tehsil. A police station had also been set-up to keep a watch over them. The Bawariyas were harassed not only by the Uttar Pradesh Police but also by the Haryana Police. Whenever a theft, burglary or dacoity was committed in the border areas of Haryana and Uttar Pradesh, the Bawariya youths would be arrested, and cases lodged. Some of their leaders, came to see me, with an activist lawyer called Kashyap, and suggested that if the administration could help their youths in getting jobs, improve their living by undertaking economic measures, it would transform their lives.

I discussed this issue with my officers as well as the Superintendent of Police. All were of the view that the administration should carry out a programme of economic upliftment of the Bawariyas. We visited the area and called all the Bawariyas for a collective discussion on their problems. Issues were raised and the departmental officers suggested solutions. I knew that I had them on board.

In the next couple of months, agricultural plots were allotted to many, jobs were given to the educated, both in Revenue and Police Departments. Tube wells were sanctioned for irrigation and additional power distribution lines were laid out. The young boys and girls were encouraged to go to schools. The girls were motivated not only to get educated but also learn vocational skills. A small soap factory was also sanctioned. Transformation gradually took place. Statistically, crime in the neighbouring areas went down.

The then Governor Reddy, visited Muzaffarnagar and I took him to interact with the Bawariyas. He came back, extremely pleased, and sent me a congratulatory letter, which I cherish. For this work, I was also awarded the Best District Magistrate Prize in 1974, along with some others.

These welfare measures are still continuing but sporadically. All the District Magistrates, who came after me, have shown positive interest in the programmes. I still go every year to Shamli (which has become a district) to review the progress and it gives me great satisfaction. One of the Bawariya youth, Jeet Ram, who had been appointed as a Lekhpal, got promoted to become a Naib Tehsildar. He has now taken over the leadership of his community and with the help of Kashyap, is making strenuous efforts to improve the image of the Bawariyas.

In Muzaffarnagar, I enjoyed holding camps in the least accessible rural areas. The Khadar area, near the river, was one such areas. I used to stay overnight in these winter camps and thus had a chance to acquaint myself with the problems of the villages. In one such camp, a villager brought me his horse and asked me if I would like to ride it. I took up the challenge. But as soon as I sat on the horse, it bolted off. The local SHO, was afraid that I might fall off, took to his jeep and raced after me. As I approached the village, people thought the police were chasing a dacoit. They cried out, *"Dakait, Dakait"* and started to chase me. We were approaching an octroi barrier, and to save me, the octroi personnel opened the gate and I went through safely. The horse went through the market place and then suddenly stopped, facing a wall. He had come to his master's courtyard! I calmly got down, put up a cool composure and sat on the police jeep. The next day, a local newspaper, *Muzaffarnagar Bulletin*, carried out a story on how a District Magistrate became a dacoit!

There were immense floods in the district in 1975. Several villages got flooded. One village literally got washed away and all the houses collapsed due to incessant rainfall. The inhabitants escaped to the other side of the river. I rushed to the village and met all the affected people. The villagers wanted to settle down in the new area. I directed the SDO to allot them residential plots on this side, while their agricultural lands remained on the original sites. Later, after many years, when I visited the village, I learnt that in the revenue records this new village has been named as 'Yogendranagar' on the request of the villagers.

Similarly, in Muzaffarnagar city, a colony was constructed and named 'Yogendrapuri'. I had no hand at all, in the naming as I was not there! But, I realized, that people do have a way of showing their affection and love.

Muzaffarnagar was a highly politically sensitive district. The ruling Congress Party, was itself divided into two groups in the district – one led by Virendra Verma, and the other by Narain Singh.

HN Bahuguna, Chief Minister of Uttar Pradesh, favoured Narain Singh and also got him appointed as Deputy Chief Minister of the State. Virendra Verma, had been very close to Chaudhary Charan Singh, former Chief Minister of Uttar Pradesh and was senior to Narain Singh, but had been put in a junior position as only a minister. There was intense rivalry between the two as one represented the Jats and the other the Gujjars.

At the time of the elections for the Cooperatives, the supporters of Virendra Verma were constantly filing complaints against the candidates of Narain Singh. Since the voting was scheduled to take place immediately, following the nominations on the next day. I had to sit late hours, dictating orders to finalize the list of candidates. Invariably I found the objections baseless and kept on rejecting them. Virendra Verma was very annoyed, as he felt that I was rejecting the complaints on the behest of Narain Singh. Virendra Verma complained to the Chief Minister, who in turn merely informed Narain Singh and took no other action.

This constant tussle between the two, hampered the work of the district administration. However, since I had directed all my officers to strictly abide by the rules, both the leaders could say nothing. Eventually Virendra Verma became very fond of me, to the extent of recommending my continuation as District Magistrate of Muzaffarnagar.

In Muzaffarnagar I came in contact with a firebrand. A youth activist, Muneesh Kumar, used to spearhead a number of agitations. My predecessor, Bahadur, was a gentle soft spoken person and Muneesh Kumar took full advantage. It is said that he had once got on top of the DM's table and shouted.

When Muneesh came to see me, I was fully prepared. Muneesh Kumar narrated a number of cases in which administration had taken no action on genuine complaints. I noted down all his complaints and asked him to come on a particular day. In the meantime I got all these complaints examined. On finding one complaint to be true, I suspended the concerned official. On the fixed date when Muneesh came I gave him my feedback on all the issues raised by him. He thanked me and also invited to me to his village. Next week I went to his village. There was no road connecting his village to the main road. I sanctioned a road to be built by *shramdan* (voluntary labour). I myself participated in the construction of the road. Muneesh Kumar was completely won over. I then advised him to take up all such issues in a peaceful manner in future. I must confess that he became a changed man thereafter. Today he has made a name for himself in the area of implementation of the Right to Information, women's right, implementation of the food rationing scheme for the poor etc. He has become completely Gandhian in his approach. This interaction with Muneesh taught me that agitations in society arise because of the adversarial approach of administration to local issues and a positive helpful attitude can change the tenor of public dialogue.

In a meeting of the newly elected Zila Parishads of Uttar Pradesh, HN Bahuguna stated in Lucknow that the Adhyaksha of the Parishad, was to be treated as mini Chief Minister of the district. When my new Adhyaksha came back from the meeting, he acted in a strange manner. He had been earlier a Block Pramukh. There was a wedding reception in which both of us were present. Suddenly I saw him calling me by waving his finger. I looked around and did not move. After five minutes of vigorous waving, he himself came and asked why I had not come when called. I thought to myself that it is time to end this once and for all. I frankly told him that the District Magistrate is independent and if Adhyakshaji wants to discuss any issue, he is free to see me in my office. The matter ended!

I stayed in the district till April 1976. Aparna, my daughter was born here. When Virendra Verma telephoned me, congratulated me in a rather sad voice My father had expired in Muzaffarnagar in February 1975, and I felt that I wanted a change. When the Appointment Secretary came to the district, he asked me where I wanted to go. I told him that I would like to work in the Department of Social Welfare as I wanted to continue to with the upliftment of the Bawariyas. However, I received my orders as Joint Secretary, Industries.

Within three months of my joining in Lucknow, I was appointed by the Chief Minister Narayan Dutt Tiwari, as the State's Director of Information. I had the privilege of attending all the Cabinet Meetings and then briefing the Press. Narayan Dutt Tiwari was Press sensitive. He would ring me up daily at 7 AM after reading all the newspapers and direct me to brief the journalists on certain issues. It was very pleasant, interacting with the Press. I was thoroughly enjoying my job.

But fate had different plans for me. Within three months, my successor in Muzaffarnagar, Brijendra Yadav, was in deep trouble. He was energetically pushing Sanjay Gandhi's Family Planning Programme. In order to be the first in the State, he started using the police to forcibly get people sterilized. There was only mild resistance, as Emergency was on, and the government was backing him fully.

One day, the Muslims of Khalapar mohalla, who were being forcibly taken for sterilization resisted, and this led to violence. Brijendra ordered firing by the police. About twenty-five Muslims were killed and several were reported missing. As Director of Information and Chief Censor, I was asked to black out the news and that is why very few people, outside Muzaffarnagar came to know about the incident.

Brijendra was immediately relieved of his district charge. The people of Muzaffarnagar sent a request to the Chief Minister ND Tiwari to send me back to the district. When he informed me of this request, I resisted. There had been no instance ever, of a District Magistrate going back to the same district in the same position. However, as the demand from the politicians and the people of Muzaffarnagar grew, and the district continued to be disturbed communally, I was re-appointed as District Magistrate, Muzaffarnagar for the second time.

As I proceeded to Muzaffarnagar by helicopter, I was received by various sections of the people. I had to stay in the

Inspection House, as Brijendra took some time in vacating the official bungalow. The next day I visited the affected sites. The administration had destroyed and broken houses of those who had resisted the sterilization. Tales of atrocities committed in the implementation of the Family Planning Programme, kept pouring in.

The next day the representatives of the Muslims came and asked me to visit Khalapar and get a first hand account of everything. Curfew had been imposed in the locality and a contingent of the PAC had been posted to enforce the curfew. Brijendra and the SSP warned me against going there as I would be attacked. My Muslim friends assured me that nothing of that kind would happen. They also requested that no policemen should accompany me as the police were hated by the residents of that area. I was in a quandary.

I decided to take the advice of the DIG Meerut as he was a very seasoned officer. KP Srivastava assured me that he would ensure that the police helped in the implementation of any decision I took.

I decided to take the plunge. Next day I told my Muslim friends, which included some young lawyers, that I will visit Khalapar today. They were very happy. They formed a cordon round me and we, went to meet the residents of that area in their houses. I was happily surprised to be vociferously welcomed by cries of "Zindabad, Mathur Sahib Zindabad" everywhere. Garlands were given to me as the residents simultaneously narrated the atrocities perpetuated on them. I told them that though I could not bring their dead ones back, could they accept me as a member of their family. This touched an emotional chord in all of them. Tension vanished and normal life resumed. They had only one request which, according to them, would restore complete normalcy. The PAC contingent camping in their area should be removed.

Much against the SSP's advice, the DIG on my suggestion, ordered their removal, early next morning. No untoward incident took place and normalcy came in the entire town. In the night, the entire Khalapar mohalla was lit up with *diyas* (earthen lamps) by the residents, as the people once again moved freely on the streets. As one newspaper came out with a screaming headline the next day – "Diwali in Khalapar". No other sentence could have captured the mood better.

A large number of people came to see me daily, I met all of them. All details of missing persons were noted. Compensation was given to each family which had suffered losses. Some, who were missing, came back. Faith in administration was restored. A Commission of Enquiry was set up, which took a couple of years to complete its report.

Muzaffarnagar has a large number of people from the Jain community. Once I was called to pay obeisance to three Jain *munis* who had come to visit the city. These Jain *munis* did not wear any clothes. I went with my wife to have their *darshan*. In front of the entire gathering of people, I was asked by the *munis*, whether I eat meat and whether I drink. I, honestly said "Yes". Then in front of the crowd, they asked me to give up both. I looked at my wife and then at the expectant crowd. I decided to accede to their wishes. A wave of joy swept those present in the assembly as I announced my decision.

I did not touch any of the above items for three months. Then my mother came. She had given up non-vegetarian food two decades back. She asked me a pertinent question – did you give up the drinks and meat because of your conviction or because of the compelling expectations of the crowd? I thought over the issue and came to the conclusion that it was not because of conviction but because I did not want to disappoint the people who were there. My mother then advised, I should give up only after an inner conviction compelled me to do so, otherwise it will be burdensome for me. I accepted her advice.

My most satisfying experience in Muzaffarnagar was my meeting with Swami Kalyandev. He was a social saint, who motivated people to set up educational institutions, especially for girls. Nobody knew from where he had come. He had no family. Only a dedicated disciple, Swami Omanand, who looked after all his needs. Swami Kalyandev was dedicated to spreading education in all the districts of western Uttar Pradesh. He went on to set-up more than three hundred such institutions. No person would refuse him donation for setting up an educational institution.

Swamiji would wear a torn *chadder* with a blanket. He would eat the non-cereal offerings given to him by the villagers collected from ordinary households. He would not drink water from any house. Nobody knew his age but it was rumoured that he was above hundred year. For his work he was awarded the Padma Bhushan and later the Padma Vibhushan by the Central Government. Once the Vice-President of India, late Sri Bhairon Singh Shekhawat had asked him for his torn *chadder* but Swamiji had politely refused.

Swami Kalyandev developed the Shukratal Ashram in Muzaffarnagar, which has developed as a popular tourist spot. He was an iconic figure and was a source of great inspiration for me. His foremost follower was Somansh Prakash, a thorough gentleman.

In June 1977, I was transferred back to Lucknow as Special Secretary, Home. My wife was happy that my posting as District Magistrate, Muzaffarnagar had ended and I could be with her once again. She had been staying alone in Lucknow for the last ten months.

In my new job, I was witness to a unique spectacle. While briefing the Chief Minister Ram Naresh Yadav, on a Parliament question, I saw a person standing at the door to the Chief Minister's room. This person threw a piece of paper on the table of the Chief Minister. After he left I asked the Chief Minister who was the person. The Chief Minister said that it was Mohammad Arif, an MLA and a minister. The piece of paper was his resignation. He was angry because about a week back, Shia-Sunni riots had occurred in Lucknow and the district administration had ordered firing, leading to the death of more than 15 people, but no action had been taken against the officials concerned.

By evening, late at night, I was informed that there had been a special cabinet meeting on the Shia-Sunni riots and the decision was that Sri RC Takru, District Magistrate, Lucknow would come in my place as Special Secretary, Home and I was to replace him as District Magistrate, Lucknow. While I was not too unhappy with this posting, my wife was very unhappy. She felt that as District Magistrate I would become busy again and be away from her and the family.

The SSP Lucknow was also removed and Sriram Arun was appointed in his place. Thus, a new team came to head the district administration in Lucknow.

As I sat in my new office and looked at the Board of District Magistrates of Lucknow, I was overwhelmed by the name of my illustrious predecessors. I suddenly realized that I was the first direct recruit of the IAS to be posted as the District Magistrate of Lucknow. All others had been senior officers, who after several years of service in the State service (PCS), had got promoted into the IAS at the age of fifty or above and become District Magistrate, Lucknow. It made me nervous. Could I handle Lucknow, the seat of the government, where the Chief Minister also sat, with maturity and responsibility?

However, first things first. A meeting was held in my room with all the senior officers of the district administration, including the police, and the Shia-Sunni riots were analysed. We were informed that there were almost 900 processions taken out by the Shias every year. All these processions were invariably attacked by mischievous elements amongst the Sunnis. As per past practice, policemen were posted in the houses of Sunnis located along the routes in which the Shia procession used to traverse. The Sunnis were traditionally not permitted even one procession and were highly resentful of the same. The origin of the prohibition on the Sunni processions was traced to the Nawabs of Oudh, who were all Shias and permitted processions of their community only and none of the Sunnis. Ever year the Sunnis would disrupt the Shia processions, leading to lathi-charge and firing. This was going on since the 1860s, ie from the time of the British.

In the meeting, it was decided that we would ban all these processions till an amicable settlement was reached between the Shias and Sunnis of Lucknow. The Uttar Pradesh Government was informed accordingly. The Home Secretary, late SB Saran, was shocked, as banning the traditional Moharram processions in Lucknow was inconceivable. However, the government did not intervene, and the ban decision was enforced.

However, we also wanted that the discussions with the Shias and Sunnis should continue. The leaders of both the communities told us that their followers would never allow them to sit together. It was therefore decided that the meetings would be held at the residence of the District Magistrate, after 11 o'clock in the night, in secret. Only the top leaders of the Shias and Sunnis would participate.

In these meetings, leaders of both the sects agreed that human life was more important than processions. The Shias however were afraid of the reaction in their community. The Shia leaders must show that they were in favour of continuing with the processions. A via media was thought about, to which everybody agreed. The Shias will try to take out the procession. By prior arrangements, the administration must arrest the Shias and their leaders and load them into waiting trucks. The Sunni leaders would restrain their community members from attacking the Shias as they came out from the Imambaras.

Everything was accordingly planned. However, the Shia leaders advised that policemen should not be present when the processions were stopped. Only the DM and the SSP, who would order the arrest, should be present. Buses and trucks should be there at some distance and they must proceed immediately with the Shia processionists and leave them at some distance outside the city. We agreed to go along with the suggestions.

However, on the actual day it was frightening. The Shias, in black robes, came out of the Ashfi Imambara, surrounded the two of us (SSP and myself), shouting slogans *"Hai Hussain – Hai Hussain"*. The Shia leaders asked us to call for the trucks/ buses urgently. We summoned the trucks by signs. The Shias were herded quickly inside and the trucks/buses left thereafter.

I must thank the Shia leaders for protecting us throughout, when we were surrounded by the frenzied mob.

This process was followed during my entire tenure as the District Magistrate. It was followed by my successors also. The Shia-Sunni problem substantially subsided. Attempts however continued to ensure peace amongst the two communities. During my tenure in Lucknow. I activated the civil defence setup in the city. We got enthusiastic volunteers in every locality. We decided to set-up intensive patrolling by the civil defence personnel. Anybody caught loitering in suspicious circumstances, was handed over to the police for necessary action. I myself, used to go late hours and inspect the night patrols. It was surprising to see their dedication. It led me to finally believe that in every person there is a latent urge to do something for his community and country. This urge has to be harnessed only.

As District Magistrate, Lucknow, I also started 'Janata Adalats'. We used to proceed to rural areas, with the entire team of officers of all departments, including power, irrigation, revenue, soil conservation, planning, etc, and hold camp the entire day. People, residing in the neighbouring areas, were invited to voice their grievances or give them in writing. Every complaint was noted and the concerned departmental officer was asked to submit a reply within 15 days to the applicant. The complainant was assured that if he did not get a reply within the stipulated time, he could approach me directly.

During my tenure in Lucknow, I was also informed that several criminals, who were on the run, wanted to surrender. There was an NGO involved which wanted to change their lives after their surrender. I encouraged them and personally attended such 'Surrender Camps'.

The press played an active role in disseminating all that I was doing. This helped me in earning credibility. I also adopted a village called Fattekhera in Mohanlalganj Block for all-around development. I still go there whenever I get a chance to come to Lucknow.

After serving in Lucknow for over two and a half years I felt I needed a change. There were several circulars from the Centre, inviting nominations for foreign training. I applied for all of them but was not lucky. Then a peculiar incident happened.

One day a very popular and respected saint, Baba Bhootnath invited me and my wife to visit his Ashram in the evening. I went to see him. He was sitting in a dark room in front of an idol of Deviji. After some conversation he looked at my eyes intently and said that it appears I wanted to change my job. I was surprised and said, "Yes". He then took out a ring from the air and tried to put it in my finger. It would not fit. He stated that there was a problem in getting what I wanted. But he asked me not to worry and blew on the ring. Thereafter he put the same ring on the same finger and it went smoothly in. He assured me that I will get what I wanted. Thereafter, after thanking him, I left. Subsequent events proved him right.

In May 1980, the SSP and I were participating in a panel discussion in the Lucknow University. Suddenly we received a message from the Home Secretary Khodai that we should rush to the airport, where the plane of the Union Home Secretary HM Patel, was force-landed for re-fuelling. We were also asked to take some food for Patel and his staff. We had the meal packets prepared in Kwality and rushed to Amausi Airport.

We remained with HM Patel for two hours at the airport, walking on the tarmac. He discussed various issues. Before embarking, he asked us, whether we would like to apprise him of any problem we were facing.

At that time I was very keen to go abroad. My name had been forwarded to the Central Government in the Home Ministry thrice but every time somebody would be selected from Delhi. I thought this was an opportune time to raise the issue. I informed HM Patel (the Department of Personnel was under him) and he promised to look into it.

After a week, I was surprised to receive a letter signed by Patel, expressing his thanks for looking after him in Lucknow. In the end he wrote that he had noted my complaint about foreign assignments and was having the matter enquired into. The next day my Home Secretary RC Thakur telephoned me, enquiring what I had complained to the Home Minister. I explained to him the entire sequence of events. Within a week my nomination for foreign training arrived *suo moto*.

During my entire tenure in Lucknow I did not ever receive any telephone or recommendation from the Chief Minister Banarsi Das. I was given a free hand in administration. When Morarji Desai became the Prime Minister, some Shia leaders met him to protest against the ban on their processions. Desai visited Lucknow with his Secretary V Shankar of the ICS. After hearing the parties, they went back to Delhi. After a fortnight, Morarji Desai sent a letter to the Chief Minister advising him to permit Shia processions together with one procession of Sunnis. We knew that, in the atmosphere prevailing, it was an impractical solution and would endanger further violence amongst the two communities. The letter from the State Government endorsing the suggestion of the Prime Minister, remained in my confidential files, buried forever. We never replied to the letter. The State Government did not send any reminder.

One incident remains etched in my memory. There was a statewide agitation against the raids being carried out by the Sales Tax Department on trading establishments. One Banwari Lal Kanchal of the BJP was leading the agitation. They had locked up the Sales Tax Officers in one of the raids, and when the police went to rescue them they resorted to violence and burnt vehicles. The Magistrate on the spot ordered firing and one trader got killed. Both the SSP and I rushed to control the situation. Curfew was imposed and I sat in one of the city *thanas*, the whole night. Next day the traders requested for permission to take out the body in a procession. Our information was that they wanted to place the body in front of the Council House. I called their leaders for discussion, and they promised that they would take the body straight to the cremation ground. Our Home Secretary advised me not to give permission. But I told him that I had been assured by the leaders, whom I trusted, that nothing untoward would happen and I would take responsibility. The procession was permitted and the leaders kept their word.

In March 1980, the General Elections were held. Prior to that, the Congress staged demonstrations against the State Government. The Youth Congress leaders tried to storm the State Secretariat and I had to be personally present as the barricades put up by the police were proving ineffective. A lathi-charge had to be resorted to. Sanjay Singh led the Youth Congress workers. From jail he telephoned me and hurled the choicest abuses. I controlled myself and merely said, "same to you."

During the Congress agitation, I perforce had to arrest Kamlapati Tripathi, ND Tiwari, Mohsina Kidwai and a host of other Congress leaders. But these senior leaders were most cooperative. They asked me to put my arm on their shoulders and voluntarily sat in the waiting cars. Many of them also seated themselves in my vehicle and I quietly asked the Magistrate present to take them to the jail. There was no animosity on either side.

Next day I got a telephone call from ND Tiwari asking whether he could get the daily newspapers. I said 'certainly' and enquired whether he needed anything else. He replied that he would not like to be given anything which his other colleagues were not getting. This was the greatness of the leaders of that time.

On receiving my orders for the foreign training in Glasgow, I did my packing and reserved my seats on the train for proceeding to Delhi. AK Rastogi was appointed as my successor in the district and I was appointed as Special Secretary, Irrigation. This enabled my family to get a government accommodation in Butler Palace Colony.

On reaching the railway platform on my date of departure, I found the platform extremely crowded. There was a massive turnout of the public of Lucknow to bid me farewell. There were people of all communities and from all walks of life – Shias, Sunnis, Sikhs, Christians, businessmen, educationists, artists, apart from my magistrates and police officers. The entire platform resounded with the shouting of my name. I was profusely garlanded. Each one of them wanted to shake hands with me. The coach in which I was to sit, was decorated with flowers. The police came in full strength and gave me a guard of honour. My service colleagues also came in large numbers. I was overwhelmed with this show of love and affection. With difficulty and moist eyes, I, my wife and children entered the coach.

As the wheels of the train rolled, I kept on waving my hands, in response to the shouting of the crowd. It gave me immense satisfaction to know that I was the recipient of so much love from the people of Lucknow.

From Delhi I flew to Glasgow to study for my Diploma in Development Economics. I was on a scholarship of the British Council who paid me a pittance of 269 pounds per month which included my house rent also. The apartment I had taken had a coin box for supplying electricity. Whenever, I needed electricity I had to put a fixed amount of coins in the box otherwise the electric supply was disconnected. To avoid spending on electricity, I would stay in the University Library till late hours. The Library was comfortably warm. This way I saved enough money to enable me to buy a return ticket for my wife Neena, from Delhi to Glasgow and back. By the time Neena came, I had cultivated an Indian petrol pump owner to give her a job as a petrol pump attendant. It was illegal but she was getting as much salary as my scholarship. Both of us saved enough to do a coach tour of Europe and a round trip to the USA to visit my sisters.

On coming back to UK, I was informed by my Professor in Glasgow University that I had been awarded the First Prize for topping in the Diploma examinations. That was the result of sitting the extra hours in the University Library.

On my return to India, I received my orders for my posting as Secretary Irrigation in the Government of Uttar Pradesh. I was thrilled. This was my first posting as Secretary. When I reached Lucknow, the Chief Secretary rang me to say that I should wait, as revised orders were to be issued. I waited for two days. Then the revised orders came. I was appointed not only as Secretary, Irrigation but also as Secretary, Power. This was a unique posting. About twenty years back, only BB Lal, ICS, had held the combined post. The two departments were held by separate Secretaries, since then, but had now been combined again. My Irrigation Minister was Veer Bahadur Singh. My Power Minister was Sunil Shastri, son of late Lal Bahadur Shastri. The Chief Minister was VP Singh.

I took this opportunity to visit all the power installations including the hydroelectric projects in the hills. These were marvels of skill and engineering. The irrigation projects with their long winding channels had brought prosperity to our rural areas. I began admiring our engineers who had developed the State.

One day the Speaker, Sripati Mishra called me to explain the problem of the irrigation channel passing through his village. There was massive water-logging on both sides of the channel, rendering the fields unproductive. He wanted the irrigation department to sort out the problem.

Those days a fresh experiment of lining irrigation channels with polythene was being carried out, to prevent loss of water due to seepage. I directed the irrigation department to carry out the experiment in the constituency of the Speaker. The experiment was successful. The Speaker was impressed and thanked me profusely.

In 1981 the Speaker became the Chief Minister. I suddenly got orders, posting me as Secretary to the Chief Minister.

Sripati Mishra was a very simple person. A practising lawyer in the district of Sultanpur, he had suddenly been elevated to the highest post in the State administration. He called me one day and said that he expected me to handle the administrative side while he handled the political side. While working I found that a large number of files were being sent for the Chief Minister's approval, even if, there was not an iota of a chance that he would disagree. I took the Chief Minister in confidence and asked him whether I could clear such files, by writing that the "Chief Minister has approved" as the files were piling up. He readily agreed. Thereafter, there was no delay in the disposal of files. The officers were happy that there was no delay now in the Chief Minister's office.

However, one day a file came from the Chief Secretary in which, he had written a long note recommending change of portfolios between two ministers. I presumed that this proposal would have come after discussions between the Chief Minister and the Chief Secretary and wrote, "The Chief Minister has approved." I never realized the political implications. Next day the newspapers were full of headlines that a minister had been relieved of his portfolio on the orders of the Chief Minister. Sripati Mishra talked to the Chief Secretary. The notification had already been issued. The Chief Minister defended 'his' decision before the press.

Once Sripati Mishra was invited to Dubai in connection with an official programme. I accompanied him. He had a seat in the First Class while I had mine in the Economy Class. I noticed, from my seat, that the air hostess was offering him drinks. I was about to intervene and inform her that the Chief Minister doesn't drink, when I saw the Chief Minister lift a glass of wine. I sat back. After five minutes, he took another glass of wine and then a third time.

When we landed at Dubai, his legs were a bit wobbly. I hastened to support him. I did not know whether the instability was due to his frail health or the drinking binge!

A representation came from the employees unions that they should get Dearness Allowance at the same rate as the Central Government employees. The Finance Department had strongly opposed the request as it felt that the State could not afford it. The Chief Minister convened a meeting of officials – the Chief

Secretary SD Srivastava, the Finance Secretary, and the Secretary of the Secretariat Administration Department. Intensive discussions followed and I was noting down all the points. Suddenly the Chief Minister turned around to look at me and said that I should also give my views. I was reluctant and said that the Chief Secretary and Finance Secretary had already advised him. But when the Chief Minister insisted, then I stated, that I have a different view. I said that the Dearness Allowance is given to compensate for the increased cost of living and when a State Government employee goes shopping he has to pay the same increased cost as a Central Government employee. Therefore the Dearness Allowance should be the same. This appealed to the Chief Minister who, in retrospect, I feel had already made up his mind and was only looking for a supporting argument. He agreed with my view point, much to the annoyance of both the Chief Secretary and the Finance Secretary. Since then the State Government employees get Dearness Allowance at the same rates as the Central Government employees.

Sripati Mishra was fond of *Paan Masala* and tobacco. On and off he used to get unwell. Once he was advised to get hospitalized in Delhi. Several medical tests followed as he continued to be in hospital. Prime Minister Indira Gandhi came to see him. She found him frail and weak. Within a week Sripati Mishra was replaced by Narayan Dutt Tiwari. Sripati Mishra had completed more than two and a half years as Chief Minister. A commendable record indeed.

He was a politician with deep insight. Once, I remember telling him that the frequent transfers of officers was not good for governance and that they must have a fixed tenure. He turned around and said "Yogendra, when even Chief Ministers don't have fixed tenures how do you expect the officers to have a fixed tenure." I became quiet.

I had worked under ND Tiwari, when he was my Finance Minister. My officers working in the Chief Minister's secretariat were not sure whether they would continue or be replaced. We decided to see the Chief Secretary Girish Mehra. He advised us that Secretary to the Chief Minister is not a political post and that he had already talked to the Chief Minister who wanted us to continue as before.

ND Tiwari had always been a courteous, polite and considerate person. Once, when I was working as Joint Secretary, Finance under him in 1972, I had sent him a note in Hindi (in Uttar Pradesh all official work is done in Hindi), recommending acceptance of a Muslim officer's request to divorce his wife. Instead of writing 'Talaq' in Hindi I wrote 'Takal'. He corrected the word in his own handwriting, saying that the Joint Secretary probably meant 'Talaq' and approved the proposal. He was polite to a fault.

In the initial months, whenever ND Tiwari would finalise proposals for transfers, he would ask me to take the file to VP Singh for his suggestions. This went on for some time till VP Singh told me not to bring any more files to him, as it was not the accepted practice and he had nothing to do with the running of the government.

Often, ND Tiwari would fly to Delhi at short notice. Once when I was seeing a movie in a theatre, near the Secretariat, with my wife, I was called by the Chief Minister. I told my wife that I will come back shortly and left her to continue seeing the movie. I never returned to the theatre as Tiwari asked me to accompany him to Delhi by the state plane. My wife returned home alone, naturally very angry.

Tiwari was dedicated to development. Often in the night around 9 PM he would take me to inspect the construction of the roads in Lucknow. He had emphasized on transparency. So, wherever work was being undertaken, there would be a board showing the cost of the construction, the details of the project and the Junior Engineer in-charge of the work.

Two interesting incidents occurred in the time of ND Tiwari. Once he asked me to go to Delhi to take the approval of the Governor on the list of ministers of the reconstituted Cabinet. When I went to see the Governor in the Uttar Pradesh Bhawan, VK Saxena, Secretary to the Governor took the file inside and asked me to wait. After some time the Governor called me inside and asked whether IB clearance on each minister had been taken. I informed him that there was no such practice and it was not done in this case either. Then he put his finger on one of the names and said you know what is her reputation? I said no. He said that she is reputed to flirt with anyone who shakes hands with her. I said shall I inform the Chief Minister. The Governor looked at me and said, "No. Tell the Chief Minister that I have approved the proposal," and handed the file to me, duly signed.

In another case when Narayan Dutt Tiwari was appointed as Chief Minister, a list of ministers to be appointed, was received from Delhi. On going through the list we found that one of the names proposed for Home Minister was that of a person who was in league with petty criminals. The Home Secretary and I went to the Chief Minister to apprise him of the position. The Chief Minister changed the portfolio. The concerned person kept on ringing me up to find out what has happened. I kept quiet!

On October 31, 1984, news of the death of Prime Minister Indira Gandhi came. An alert was sounded. ND Tiwari wanted to leave for Delhi immediately and participate in the funeral. I rushed to my office. Telephones lines were clogged. I had the

Chief Minister's office opened. On the RAX I got the Resident Commissioner, Uttar Pradesh on the line and informed him about the Chief Minister's programme. Our State Plane was ready. The Chief Minister said that he would be going alone and asked me to keep a watch on the situation in the State. There was a fear of anti-Sikh riots all over the country. The Home Secretary and DGP had been alerted.

The Chief Secretary talked to all the Commissioners and informed them about the situation. By evening riots had been averted, except in one district, Kanpur where the District Magistrate was not complying with the orders of the government. He was doing nothing to protect the Sikhs. The Chief Secretary was getting desperate calls for help from the Sikhs in Kanpur. The Chief Secretary was repeatedly directing the District Magistrate Kanpur, Brijendra Yadav, to act firmly against those who were attacking the Sikhs. However, Brijendra was under the influence of the local leaders of Kanpur, who were seeking revenge against the Sikhs for killing their leader, Indira Gandhi. Since the District Magistrate was refusing to act, he was replaced and the situation in Kanpur came under control only after three-four days.

In the meantime the rioting in Delhi had continued. Reports of Sikhs being killed were coming in through newspapers. However, because of the firm stand of the Uttar Pradesh administration, the situation remained under control in Uttar Pradesh.

Once while staying in Uttar Pradesh Bhawan in Delhi, a woman, came in the late hours, saying that she wanted to see Tiwariji immediately. As the Chief Minister had retired for the day, the lady was advised to come the next day. She refused to go and asked the Chief Minister's PS to go and inform the Chief Minister that she had come with his child. The PS was perplexed but informed the Chief Minister accordingly. ND Tiwari came out immediately and asked us all to leave. Later we learnt that this lady and her son went to court, and ND Tiwari was subsequently forced to accept her as his wife.

Neither Sripati Mishra nor ND Tiwari ever involved us in political matters. Once I remember, during the elections, Shiv Shankar, minister at the Centre, came to discuss election strategy for Uttar Pradesh. He was also carrying some bags of notes. Tiwari asked us to leave, saying that the presence of officers was not required as he was engaged in political work. This was how the politicians worked in those days.

Chapter 4

My First Experience in Delhi

I HAD given my name for a Central posting and in May 1985 I received my orders to join as Joint Secretary in the Ministry of Shipping and Transport. ND Tiwari asked me to suggest a name to fill my vacancy. I recommended the name of my batchmate Ravindra Mathur, who happened to be the Chief Minister's choice also. Ravindra was hard-working and could get along with everybody.

In Delhi, my Secretary in the Ministry of Surface Transport was Prakash Narain, a lovable and a very affable person, very knowledgeable in the field of transport. My minister Ansari was a gentleman from Unnao. He used to recite Urdu poetry at the drop of a hat. He loved his pan and tobacco like most ministers coming from Uttar Pradesh. After a couple of years, he was replaced by Rajesh Pilot, a young and dynamic minister, a complete contrast to Ansari.

In those days, DTC was looked after by the Ministry. The DTC employees raised some unreasonable demands and threatened to go on strike. Rajesh Pilot called me and requested me to go to Lucknow and see if they could send some 200 buses of Uttar Pradesh Roadways to Delhi to help in breaking the strike.

I proceeded to Lucknow. Jagdish Khattar, who was my batchmate, was also Transport Secretary, Uttar Pradesh. He was immensely helpful. He not only put me up in his house but arranged the buses. Within a week, the buses had started coming to Delhi. The citizens of Delhi were not inconvenienced at all and the DTC strike was a complete failure. They requested for negotiations and withdrew the strike. Rajesh Pilot praised me a lot for the swift action. But I always remained grateful to Jagdish Khattar for his help.

As Joint Secretary, Ports, I was directly looking after the construction of the Nhava Sheva Port in New Bombay. Mrs Anna Malhotra, a senior IAS officer and wife of the former RBI Governor Sri Malhotra, was appointed as Chairman of the new port. She was a dynamic lady, extremely hard-working, dedicated to her job and with a no nonsense outlook. Within five years, the port of Nhava Sheva was ready and renamed as Jawaharlal Nehru Port. It proved that with proper leadership, it was possible to achieve anything in India.

My mother expired in the midnight of 26th and 27th January 1987. I was participating in the Board meeting of the Bombay Port Trust when I got the news. My brother Surendra Narain Mathur, was working in Bombay at that time. Both of us took the first flight to Delhi early in the morning. After the cremation, I remembered that my mother had told me that after her death, I should open a letter which she had left for me in her cupboard. I opened the letter. Amongst other instructions, she had written that she wanted her ashes to be immersed in all the four Dhams ie Badrinath, Dwarka, Rameshwaram and Puri. I complied with her instructions and this gave me an opportunity to visit all the Dhams.

My Additional Secretary in the Ministry was PM Abraham. Extremely affectionate, hard-working and methodical. He was clear in his views. I learnt a lot from him. He taught me the art of writing notes on files. Each line had to be supported by facts and logic. He was from Kerala and gave me a free hand. I was also the Vigilance Officer of the Ministry. Saifulla, the Chairman of the Bombay Port Trust, was also under vigilance surveillance. He later became the Cabinet Secretary. Saifulla used to come late in the evenings and embarrass me by requesting me to show files relating to his case. I had to be extremely diplomatic in saying no. It is the failure of the system, that in spite of vigilance enquiries against him, he became the Cabinet Secretary after some years.

In my time TN Seshan was the Cabinet Secretary. He was the author of a bizarre plan which evolved to foil the attempt of the Secretariat employees to go on strike in 1988. He directed all the Ministries to issue orders directing all the employees to stay back in the Ministry throughout the night and continue working till the next day. We also had to stay back and arrange food for the employees. I was made the nodal officer of my Ministry to organize the stay-in. Next day Seshan told the Prime Minister that there was hundred per cent attendance and the strike had failed!

Once Rajiv Gandhi went for holidays with his family and friends to Lakshadweep. It took him three days on the ship to reach the islands. As a pilot he was not used to such delays. Immediately after coming back, he directed that it should be quickly examined whether an airport could be set up in Lakshadweep together with some berths for shipping. Anil Baijal and myself were sent with technical personnel to study the situation on the spot. We went there. Subsequently

Lakshadweep got connected by air and has become an attractive tourist centre.

Some time at the end of 1989, the Bombay Port Trust workers went on strike. The Cabinet Secretary, Sri Seshan convened meetings every evening to review the strike situation. The Bombay Port Trust Chairman who had come in about a year back, was showing softness to the employees and was slow in taking action against them. PM Abraham decided to replace him. The next day Seshan questioned the decision to replace him. Under his ferocious demeanour any other Secretary would have backed out. Such was the reputation of Seshan! But not PM Abraham. He bluntly told Seshan that he (Abraham) was the Secretary of the Department and knew his officers well. The Chairman of the Port Trust must go! Seshan backed down. PM Abraham had called Seshan's bluff. Seshan was a bully and like all bullies he had backed down when he met his match!

In Seshan's tenure as Cabinet Secretary, another very interesting incident occurred. Prime Minister Rajiv Gandhi had been slighted by the King of Nepal in a meeting abroad. PM Abraham, my Secretary in the Surface Transport Ministry, received orders from the Cabinet Secretariat that the Prime Minister has ordered that the berth in Calcutta port, which was reserved for the transit of goods to landlocked Nepal, should be decommissioned. When PM Abraham passed on these orders to me, in my capacity as Joint Secretary Ports, I immediately spoke to the then Chairman, Calcutta Port Trust and asked him to have the orders implemented. Chairman, Calcutta Port Trust replied that as this is against international law he would not be able to implement the orders. When I reported back to the Secretary, he discussed the matter with the Cabinet Secretary, but was rebuffed by Seshan who said,

"The Prime Minister desires that these orders be implemented at once."

I again talked to the Chairman, Calcutta Port Trust, who bluntly told me, that he would do so, only if he got the orders in writing from the Ministry. I discussed the matter once again with the Secretary on the request of the Chairman. The Secretary asked me to sort out the matter discreetly. I told the Chairman of the Calcutta Port Trust that I would send the letter conveying these orders to him, but requested him to keep it locked in his safe and personal custody. If ever the Chairman got into any problem on this issue, he would be at liberty to show the letter in his defence. To this, the Chairman agreed.

The berth, earmarked for Nepal, was temporarily closed on account of 'silting'. The Nepalese Ambassador visited me almost every day as the ships with goods for Nepal were waiting at the port. This went on for three weeks, by which time Nepal relented at the highest level, and the matter arising out of the insults to our Prime Minister was amicably settled. The berth was opened once again as the 'de-silting', by coincidence also got completed!

As my five year deputation was ending in 1990. I wrote a letter to the Chief Secretary, Uttar Pradesh, asking the State Government's permission to join the nine month Advanced Professional Programme in Public Administration (APPPA) in IIPA. After obtaining permission I joined the course. It was very satisfying. I had practised Public Administration but had not learnt the theory of administration. I was exposed to the evolving principles of governance for the first time.

I did my MPhil on a topic unknown in India then – 'Right to Information'. I had heard about this subject in the USA.

At the end of the course I was declared as the winner of the Menon Prize for topping in the course. My Director, IIPA advised me and encouraged me to join the PhD programme. I agreed to enrol myself in the IIPA/Panjab University PhD, for the subject 'Operationlisation of the Right to Information in Uttar Pradesh'.

CHAPTER 5

Back to Uttar Pradesh – Phase 2

IN the meantime on my request to post me near Delhi (I had sent a simple letter by post to the Chief Secretary, Uttar Pradesh), I was posted as the first Chairman of Greater New Okhla Industrial Development Authority (Greater Noida) which was being conceptualized, beyond the limits of the existing New Okhla Industrial Development Authority. I must thank late VK Saxena, the then Chief Secretary, for this posting. My children could continue with their education in Delhi.

Since I was the first Chairman of Greater Noida, there was no office, no telephone, no staff, no peons, etc. I realized the meaning of 'starting from scratch'. Hemendra, my colleague was the then Chairman Noida. He offered his office sofa set to sit and start my office till I got my own. He gave me a telephone and a PA. He gave me some of his officers on deputation. After two days he gave me a separate room in the office of the Noida Authority. If it was not for his helpful attitude, I could never have succeeded in establishing the Greater Noida Authority.

I had seen how the farmers had opposed land acquisition in this area. I therefore decided to visit all the Panchayats in the Greater Noida area. I talked to the Pradhans and Panchayat members. I endeavoured to convince them of the advantages of this new Authority. They replied that the Noida Authority had also promised jobs to them but nothing had happened. I began to sense that if I was to win their support I will have to prove to them that the establishment of the Authority would be to their advantage.

The local MLA Narendra Singh Bhatti, used to hold a public meeting on the 1st of every month, denouncing the Authority. I had to do something fast. I talked to the local industrialists and requested them to help the Authority by recruiting some local youths in an open manner. A Rozgar Mela was organized. All the eligible unemployed youths of the area were put in separate tents as per their qualifications. The local industrialists were then asked to go around and do 'campus recruitments'. That day more than sixty youth got their employment. It was a success!

The next day Sri Narendra Singh Bhatti came to my office and congratulated me on this initiative. He said he would henceforth support the Authority at every step. He also made a request and that was to include his area Dadri, also in the Greater Noida. I had now got his full confidence. Henceforth, land acquisition was no more a problem.

Coming fresh from the IIPA, I began trying some innovative managerial techniques. Every month I would hold a meeting with my officers and staff up to the level of the peons and chowkidars. I used to request them to give suggestions for the better running of the Authority. The suggestions I received, ranged from giving water to the villagers who come for their work in the offices, to saving electricity by ensuring the closure of lights in offices, when not needed.

My next job was to acquire land for the Authority. Government said it could not give me any money and asked me to make my own arrangements. I went to Oriental Bank of Commerce for loan. The Bank said it could give a loan on a government guarantee. I went to the government. The proposal went to the Cabinet and was rejected. I then devised another scheme. I earmarked a portion of land and advertised. Plots were offered on a deposit of ₹20,000 each. Against 2,000 plots we got 2,500 applications. I invited the allottees to come and see the area. When they came they saw green fields and many of them accused us of cheating them. I told them that if they wanted to withdraw, I would allow them to do so without any cost. Only about 200 withdrew. So, finally the Authority had some money.

But I had to raise more money for the acquisition. I went to Lucknow to see the Chairman, Board of Revenue, Anadi Sehgal. He was playing tennis. After he finished playing, I went with him to his office. I asked him whether he would permit acquisition of land on the basis of a bank guarantee. He smiled and agreed. The Board of Revenue issued orders accordingly (perhaps for the first time in its history!).

I gradually paid back the Bank from the deposits the Authority received from the applicants for the plots. Then I advertised for another sector and got more deposits. This was a new financial model I developed.

I named the first two sectors Alpha and Beta. I did not want to give names of any political leaders as I had found that, with change of regimes, names would change. I find to my surprise that this Greek nomenclature has continued even now.

One day I got a telephone call from Sri Kalyan Singh, Chief Minister that he wanted me to join as Secretary to the Chief

Minister. I was asked to come immediately to Lucknow. Sri Nripendra Misra, Secretary to the Chief Minister, was posted in my place as Chairman, Greater Noida. I thus proceeded to take my assignment for the third time as Secretary to the Chief Minister.

The State plane took me to Lucknow. Sri Kalyan Singh, who had to go for a function in one of the districts outside Lucknow was waiting for me at the airport to welcome me. He had delayed his departure. I was overwhelmed by his courtesy and affection.

The atmosphere in Lucknow was surcharged with the developments relating to the Babri Masjid. Both the Central Government and the State Government had given an assurance to the Supreme Court that they would protect the Babri Masjid. On the other hand the Kar Sewaks were coming to Ayodhya from all over the country. There was no way of stopping them from going to Ayodhya. Police did search them to ensure that no arms were being carried. Every day the gathering of Kar Sewaks was increasing. The Supreme Court was keeping a watch on the situation and taking an assurance from the State Government that all precautions to protect the Babri Masjid had been taken.

One day Kalyan Singh went to Delhi to see the Prime Minister Narasimha Rao. I accompanied him to the Prime Minister's residence. While I sat outside, both of them proceeded inside. After an hour Kalyan Singh came out and sat in the car with me. He turned to me and said, "Yogendra, do you know what the Prime Minister told me." I looked at him. The Prime Minister told me that the ASI had, in the course of its digging under the Babri Masjid as per directions of the Supreme Court, actually found remnants of a temple at the location. This confirmed the fact that the Babri Masjid, had been built after razing a temple on that place. I was surprised but Kalyan Singh felt quite relieved. This is what his party had been saying always.

As the Kar Sewaks gathered at Ayodhya, the Central Government rushed Central para-military forces to the temple town. The strength of the central forces increased day by day as did the strengths of the Kar Sewaks. It was an explosive situation under the watch of the Supreme Court, the Central Government, the State Government as well as the Muslim and Hindu communities.

Then came 6th December 1992.

The Chief Minister, together with Lalji Tandon and Sri Om Prakash Singh were closeted together in front of a TV in the Chief Minister's house. I sat outside the Chief Minister's room. Lunch was served to all of them. They were glued to the TV even while they lunched. Some Kar Sewaks had got on top of the Babri Masjid. The Central forces were trying to pull them down. LK Advani and many other dignitaries were sitting on an erected platform nearby and were giving speeches.

Suddenly, we saw the Kar Sewaks started breaking the dome. The police could not rush in, because the Kar Sewaks had surrounded the structure in a thick formation.

SM Tripathi, DGP, Uttar Pradesh, came rushing to meet the Chief Minister, I informed the ministers inside. They asked him to wait till they had finished their lunch. When I conveyed this to Tripathi, he said he wanted to talk to the Chief Minister himself urgently. The Chief Minister agreed to meet him. Tripathi was straightforward. He wanted permission to open firing to prevent the Kar Sewaks from breaking the structure. Kalyan Singh asked him whether a large number of people would get killed if firing was ordered on the mob. Tripathi said,

"Yes. A large number will die in the firing." Kalyan Singh then denied him the permission to fire and asked the DGP to control the mob by any other means (like a lathi-charge, or tear gas shelling). The DGP went back to his office.

After that one could only watch on the TV, how the structure fell, brick by brick. There was no way the police and the Central forces could reach the disputed structure in view of the large number of Kar Sewaks who had surrounded it. The Central Government wanted to send the Central forces with the help of helicopters, but by that time nothing could be done. The structure had been completely dismantled.

Kalyan Singh asked for his writing pad. He wrote his letter of resignation with his own hand and proceeded to the Governor's house to deliver it personally to the Governor. By evening, news of his resignation was picked up by the TV. President's rule was announced thereafter. Governor Satyanarayan Reddy, took over the reins of the State Government.

Soon after, Sri Rajesh Pilot, State Minister for Home, Government of India, came on an official visit. He sought me out and asked where I was posted. I informed him that I was Principal Secretary, Information. He said that they should post me as Home Secretary. I requested him not do it as I had been Principal Secretary to the Chief Minister and my actions against those who perpetuated this demolition would be always viewed with suspicion. He agreed and I lay low in a non-descript position voluntarily.

I was nominated for a course in John Hopkins University, USA. In the meantime the Governor Reddy, had changed and Sri Motilal Vora, former Chief Minister of Madhya Pradesh, took charge. I got a telephone call in the USA that I had been appointed as the Principal Secretary to the Governor and on my return I have to join on that post. Sri Motilal Vora also got an officer from MP, Sri Lalit Joshi, as his OSD. I did not know either of them.

Sri Lalit Joshi was an extremely competent officer. He was very good in Hindi and wrote all the speeches for the Governor. I concentrated myself in dealing with the files coming from the various departments under President's Rule. Sri Motilal Vora was extremely courteous and polite. He was a cultured person and together with him, I introduced a monthly feature of cultural evenings in the Raj Bhawan. Several artists and Ghazal vocalists came to stay in the Raj Bhawan during that period.

Once a peculiar situation arose. Anup Jalota, the famous Ghazal singer, came for a programme to Lucknow. Sri Motilal Vora invited him to stay at the Raj Bhawan. The organizers of the programme had not taken permission from the district administration for holding the function. The District Magistrate, Lucknow had not approved the holding of the programme. When Sri Motilal Vora heard about it, he asked me to talk to the District Magistrate that he (the Governor) would also be accompanying Anup Jalota and would participate in the programme. The District Magistrate and SSP, Lucknow were in a fix. But in view of the Governor's stand, they had no option but to permit the programme to be held.

With Sri Moti Lal Vora, I did extensive tours of the districts of Uttaranchal. He was a people's man and would get down whenever and wherever people wanted him to do so. They welcomed him with garlands. He and his wife used to climb up the mountains to see people in their houses and taste their food. It was great fun and a great period of learning for me.

The Governor was a popular person. People came to see him in large numbers every day. He had great respect for the bureaucracy, specially the Chief Secretary TSR Subramaniam. But once it so happened that a leftist organization 'Sahmat' wanted to stage a street play in Ayodhya. Arjun Singh, the Union Minister wanted the Governor to give permission for the same. Ayodhya was already tense after the demolition of the Babri Masjid. The application was processed in the Secretariat and based on the advice of the DGP, the Chief Secretary recommended that the application for staging the Street play in Ayodhya should be rejected. Sri Moti Lal Vora was under intense pressure from Sri Arjun Singh and he sought my advice. The Governor also did not want to be seen as rejecting the opinion of the Chief Secretary. I pondered over the matter and thought of a solution. The Advisor to the Governor was one Bahl from Delhi. He was in-charge of the Home portfolio. I went to him and asked if he was willing to record a note recommending that permission for the street play, should be given. After hearing what the Governor wanted, he agreed but he asked me to draft a note on his behalf. I did so and after making some amendments, he signed the note. The file was put up to the Governor who readily signed the note. Thus, permission was given. TSR Subramaniam was unhappy with the decision but like a true civil servant, he told the Governor that he would fully implement the decision. It was the duty of the civil servant to advise, but once a decision is given, it is the duty of the civil servant to implement it faithfully. Needless to say the play was staged but without any public audience as the police fully surrounded the area all around!

As was inevitable, Central Government decided to hold the Assembly elections. The BJP secured the highest number of seats but without a majority. The Governor called Sri Kalyan Singh first and asked him to show proof whether he had the support of the majority of the elected MLAs. Sri Kalyan Singh asked for time which was granted. After three days he came back to the Governor saying that he could not get the requisite support. The Governor then asked the party with the next highest number of seats, i e the Samajwadi Party, whether they were in a position to form the government. Sri Mulayam Singh Yadav readily agreed. Within 24 hours, telegrams, faxes came in from various group supporting Sri Mulayam Singh Yadav in the formation of a government. A report was accordingly prepared for the Central Government and sent by flight. The approval of the President, terminating Governor's Rule, immediately came. A letter was drafted asking Sri Mulayam Singh Yadav to form the government. I personally went to deliver the letter to Sri Mulayam Singh conveying the Governor's invitation for formation of the government. Sri Mulayam Singh welcomed me at his residence and as I delivered the letter, sweets were distributed.

After the swearing in, as we were moving towards the tea reception, Sri Mulayam Singh turned to me and said that I should come as his Secretary to the Chief Minister. I told him that the Governor might not agree. Sri Mulayam Singh asked me to suggest a name. I advised him to appoint Sri Punia as his Principal Secretary. Sri Mulayam Singh readily agreed. Sri Punia was an excellent officer and knew the functioning of the government very well. He was accordingly appointed.

TSR Subramaniam continued as the Chief Secretary. But he felt uncomfortable working with Sri Mulayam Singh Yadav. There were differences on policy matters. After some months TSR Subramaniam sought a posting in the Centre and moved to Delhi.

After a few months, as the new government settled down I requested the Governor to permit me to move to Delhi as it was going to be beneficial for my career. He reluctantly agreed. At that time, the Union Cabinet Secretary Sri Surendra Singh came on an official visit to Lucknow and stayed at the Raj Bhawan. I took the opportunity to request him for a posting in Delhi. He asked me whether the Governor would agree to relieve me. I told him that I had already taken his permission. Within a month I received orders appointing me as Chairman of the National Highway Authority, a newly created post. I was asked to report to the Secretary, Ministry of Surface Transport, Government of India, Delhi. I left for Delhi with happy memories of the love and affection bestowed on me by Sri Moti Lal Vora.

Chapter 6

Experience in Delhi – Phase 2

I REPORTED to the Secretary, Ministry of Surface Transport, Sri CN Ramdas. An extremely courteous, affectionate and loving person. He welcomed me with a smile and a warm handshake. He allotted me a room in the Ministry for starting my new innings as Chairman, National Highways Authority. He also advised me that since the Authority was an autonomous body, I would soon have to find a separate office for myself.

An engineer of the National Highways Division of the Ministry, Sri Kamlesh Kumar, was deputed to the Authority to work under me. I soon learnt that because of it being an autonomous body, the Ministry would not be issuing me any stationery, pins, clips, pen stands, etc. Apart from the basic furniture, given to me temporarily to start work, no other help would be given. Even the letters would not be despatched by the concerned section in the Ministry. I found it a bit galling but this was the policy of the establishment.

Not willing to be dependent on anybody I went with Sri Kamlesh Kumar to the market and bought fountain pens, a pen stand, two packets of foolscap paper and a pin cushion out of the money allotted to the Authority. Ramdas was kind enough to allow me the use of the *dak* despatcher of the Ministry to send letters of the Authority. However, a Section Officer of the Ministry, Rawat who had worked under me in my last stint in the Ministry, was very helpful. He belonged to Uttarakhand and he assured me that whatever be the rules governing autonomous bodies, he would ensure that I got everything I wanted.

I advertised for a building to house the office of the Authority. After seeing several buildings I honed in on a building in Maharani Bagh. It was big enough to house the office as well as my residence. The rate, per square metre, was the lowest I could have got in Delhi. I wrote a note and got approval of the Secretary. Soon I moved into this building. We also made the logo for NHAI.

I wanted the Authority to be lean and thin. I therefore took officers mainly on deputation from the Ministry and later from the States. Further, as a policy, I wanted to work with the aim of eventually establishing a paperless office. So, computers came in a big way, right from the beginning. Privatization was being encouraged in all infrastructure areas. Sri Kamlesh Kumar and I also started to examine how privatization could be encouraged in the national highway sector. There was a big crunch on finances and apart from the nominal grant from the budget, the Ministry was very reluctant to release additional funds to me, as they were also getting less than their requirement.

My minister was now Sri Jagdish Tytler. He was very helpful. He asked me to accompany him to Malaysia, which had developed the famous North-South Expressway, connecting North Malaysia to South Malaysia. We signed an MoU with them for cooperation in the highway sector.

Thereafter, I went on an official visit to examine how Malaysia had constructed the famous North-South Expressway. It was a surprise for me to see the polished and well maintained highway. There were also resting places every fifty kilometres with fuel stations, children's recreation points, toilets and canteen. We had none of this in India. I also saw modern new road construction machines, which had speeded up construction of the highways. There were also toll plazas all along the highway which substantially contributed to the coffers.

The country I next went to study was the USA. Seeing the impressive six- and eight-lane highways in the USA, I asked a US National Highway department officer who was accompanying me, as to where do they get these huge funds for building these excellent roads. For the first time I learnt that the US Government had a policy of imposing a cess on every gallon of gasoline (petrol) bought by the car owners. This helped them to collect a large amount of funds which were reinvested in maintenance and construction of highways. I decided to introduce this in India. I also saw the most modern highway construction machines in the world which had helped the US in rapid construction of highways.

Soon after coming back to India, I wrote a note to the Secretary of the Surface Transport Ministry proposing a fifty paise cess on every litre of petrol and diesel sold in India. I then started advocating this cess, in every meeting of the Chambers of Commerce, FICCI, Assocham, wherever I was invited. I recommended this step to offset the cash crunch that was facing the road sector in India.

To encourage privatization, Kamlesh Kumar came forward with a brilliant idea of building new highways connecting the North-South, East-West and the coastal areas of India (what he called the Golden Quadrilateral) with the help of the private sector. I was very excited. In an interview with *The Economic Times*, a map of the proposal Golden Quadrilateral was published for the first time in 1996. We also invited expressions of interest and eleven bidders came forward. This plan had obviously excited the construction agencies involved in the infrastructure areas.

I sent the proposal to the Ministry for approval. They in turn sent it to the Ministry of Finance. I was called for a meeting in the Finance Ministry to discuss the proposal. After lengthy discussions they shot down the proposal saying it was a risky new area. They also stated that the World Bank had expressed interest in funding the infrastructure area and therefore we should take funds from them rather than invite the private sector. We in the Authority returned sad and depressed.

In the meantime, Cabinet Secretary TSR Subramaniam was giving a big thrust to infrastructure development. He was taking a large delegation of officers involved in the infrastructure sector like ports, road, shipping, power, inland water ways, to the USA to give a presentation to the construction giants and invite them to participate in infrastructure development projects in India. I was also asked to be part of the delegation and give a presentation on highway development. I utilized this opportunity and exhibited our national highway development plan through a power point presentation. I believe it was well received.

The NHAI was entrusted with the four-laning of the Delhi-Jaipur Highway. After the four laning was completed we sent a proposal for tolling of the complete highway. There were many doubting Thomas's who felt that tolling would not succeed and nobody would pay. We commissioned a study to find out what would be a reasonable and acceptable toll rate for the commuters. Based on the study, we sent a proposal to the Ministry for approval. After taking approval of the Cabinet, the Ministry sent us a formal go ahead. We then started constructing the toll plazas. The toll collection rights were auctioned, and on the basis of the highest bid, the contractor was approved. No untoward incident took place and everybody paid the tolls without a demur. This was the first toll collection to be auctioned on National Highways and set the precedent for the rest of the country.

AD Narain had become the new DG Roads in the Ministry. He had fully supported my proposal of charging toll on National Highways. I remember that in a function, the then Minister of Surface Transport, Sri Venkataraman stated that he expected both the Narains (AD Narain and myself) to rid the problems of *Daridra Narayan* (the weaker section) from the country. The minister had become very fond of me. The retirement of Sri Sunder, Secretary, Surface Transport, was due within a month. The minister sent for me and asked me to see the Cabinet Secretary. He directed me to tell the Cabinet Secretary that he wants me as the next Secretary of the Ministry. I told him that it was not proper for me to carry this message and he could talk to the Cabinet Secretary himself. The minister however insisted.

I went to the Cabinet Secretary in the afternoon and in great embarrassment gave him the message. However, TSR Subramaniam, who had been my Chief Secretary in Uttar Pradesh, just smiled and said nothing. After a week, orders were received appointing me as the Secretary of the Surface Transport Ministry.

I took charge as Secretary of the Ministry on 1st April 1997. The Truck Drivers Federation had given a call for strike, a fortnight earlier and this was my first challenge. Some papers were critical of the change of guard at this crucial moment. I called the Federation leaders for talks. Some of the demands related to the insurance premium in which the Secretary, Insurance was involved. The other demands related to government taxes. After negotiations, in which both the Finance Secretaries were also involved. I sent a draft agreement to NK Singh, Joint Secretary, Ministry of Finance who was coordinating on behalf of the Finance Secretary to get the approval of the Finance Minister P Chidambaram. I received a reply from NK Singh by FAX that the Finance Minister has approved the draft agreement.

I informed the Federation leaders and they were also very happy. The signing was to take place in the Finance Minister's room. When I went there, I was aghast at the attitude of the Finance Minister. He said that the agreement had been wrongly drafted and that he would never sign on such an agreement. I looked at NK Singh but he preferred to remain quiet. Later, when I met him outside, he said that as he was only looking after Insurance, he had got that paragraph approved and not the full agreement.

The Federation leaders were waiting for the signing ceremony to take place. The TV channels had also come. I told the Federation leaders that the Finance Minister had certain reservations and wanted some portions of the agreement deleted. They were also taken aback.

However, the leader of the Federation was from Kanpur. He knew me well as I had helped him while I was in Uttar Pradesh. He told his men to consider the revised proposal with a cool mind. He argued with them on my behalf and the agreement was revised.

Sri Chidambaram, who was quite angry, was threatening to go back to his house. I went with a revised draft. He went through it and approved. Doordarshan was called. The agreement was signed and the nationwide truck drivers' strike was called off. I thanked the truck owners for their cooperation, who in return thanked me for all the efforts made for their welfare.

From the Finance Minister's room I went straight to the Ashoka Hotel where I had arranged a farewell party for Sunder. I was already one hour late. I apologized for the delay and explained the entire situation to him. He was quite understanding and congratulated me on successfully calling off the strike.

We had a very understanding minister from the South – Venkataraman. He always supported me and work went on very smoothly. The Prime Minister at that time was IK Gujral. TSR Subramaniam, who was keen to fast track the development of infrastructure in India, discussed with the Secretaries of the infrastructure ministries to give a presentation to the Prime Minister in the Cabinet and obtain decisions on pending issues. My team worked hard and prepared a PowerPoint presentation, and after showing it to our minister, put it up to the Prime Minister in the Cabinet. As I was explaining the issues involved, Gujral asked whether the Environment Ministry was holding up clearances. I said that they were quite cooperative and were speeding up the process. He sat quiet but after some time, angrily remarked that he had no time to go through the presentation and that I should raise only the issues requiring his decision. He then got up angrily and said that he had another meeting to go to. After he left, I continued with my presentation. The Cabinet Secretary supported me on every issue and I got Cabinet clearance on all my proposals. I felt both disappointed and happy. Disappointed at the Prime Minister's behaviour and happy that all my proposals had got cleared. Later on, my colleague and batch mate, Vishwanath Anand, Secretary, Ministry of Environment explained why the Prime Minister was so annoyed. Apparently the Prime Minister had tried to coerce Vishy in giving clearances to certain projects. When Vishy did not oblige, he was very angry. When the Prime Minister had asked me whether my Ministry was having trouble in getting clearance from the Ministry of Environment and I said "no", Gujral was very unhappy! Vishy always repeats this incident to describe how I faced the wrath of the Prime Minister.

In 1997 I had to go to London to attend the International Maritime Conference. An unusual incident happened there. I was sleeping in my hotel room when the telephone bell rang. I picked up the telephone. The voice at the other end said that the Prime Minister wanted to talk to me. Prime Minister Gujral came on the line. He said that several people had come to him and had requested that the Delhi Haridwar road should be immediately improved as the Kumbh Mela was going to be held in Haridwar in six months. I told him that it was a State Highway and I would request the State Government to expedite the repairs. He then asked whether the Central Government could directly do something about it. I said we could do so, if we declare it a National Highway. He said, "Do it." I told him that I am coming back to India in two days and would ensure that it is done. He was surprised and asked me where I was. I told him I was in London. He apologized profusely and said that his PA had told him that I was in

Lucknow! He asked me the time in London and, profusely apologizing, closed the telephone.

I travelled extensively on National Highways in many States. Based on the Malaysian model, I introduced a provision in the National Highways Manual of having resting places with restaurants, toilets and fuel stations every fifty kilometres, I endeavoured to have more PPP projects but the model proposed for such projects used to get bogged down in the Ministry of Finance. Sri Montek Singh did not look too kindly on the PPP projects.

Chapter 7

Back to Uttar Pradesh as Chief Secretary

IN the middle of March 1998, the Cabinet Secretary Sri Prabhat Kumar, rang me up to say that the Chief Minister Sri Kalyan Singh wanted me as the Chief Secretary of Uttar Pradesh. I was reluctant as I had just moved into an independent house in Pandara Park and was enjoying my job in the Surface Transport Ministry. However, what the Cabinet Secretary wills, has to be accepted.

On 2nd April 1998 I moved over to Lucknow as Chief Secretary.

I got a very warm welcome by the officers. I called on the Chief Minister and thanked him for putting his trust in me. After the initial briefings I got onto the job.

One day as I was leaving office at 9.30 PM, I saw a journalist with his children and wife sitting on the floor. He was a Muslim and I knew him from the days I was Director of Information. On being asked why he had come at this late hour, he said that he had been evicted from his residence given to him by the Estate Department, without any notice. I went back to my office and got through to the Estate Officer and asked him whether any notice had been issued. He replied in the negative but said that he was under orders to evict him. They had thrown out his luggage and belongings on the road. I directed the Estate Officer to immediately put all his belongings back and issue him a regular notice and abide by all procedures as per law. The journalist gave his blessings and went back home.

I did extensive touring of the State. My wife used to join me often in these tours. Kalyan Singh was an admirable administrator and extremely quick in taking decisions. I decided to hold meetings with the officers in each division. In one such divisional meeting, while reviewing the road construction programmes, and maintenance of roads, all the District Magistrates complained about a particular Executive Engineer. I looked at Sri Laxmi Chand, Principal Secretary, Public Works Department, and asked him whether we could suspend the Engineer since everybody was blaming him for the neglect of the roads in the Division. Laxmi Chand said I could do so. I accordingly ordered the suspension of the Executive Engineer and also announced this in the Press Conference which followed. All the newspapers carried this story on their front pages.

After three months I happened to be sitting with the Chief Minister with some papers. He said "Yogendra, do you know that in the Agra meeting, you suspended an Executive Engineer." I said, "Yes, all District Magistrates were complaining against him." Kalyan Singh smiled and said that the Engineer was his man whom he had specially posted in Agra. "However, when I learnt that you, as Chief Secretary had suspended him, I did not intervene. I did not want to do anything to lessen the dignity of the Chief Secretary." This was the greatness of Kalyan Singh.

In 1999 eastern Uttar Pradesh was hit by floods. Gorakhpur was surrounded by the swelling rivers. There was no approach to the city. The District Magistrate and Commissioner, Gorakhpur were asking for boats but there was no way of sending them. I then contacted the AOC-in-C, Air Force, Allahabad, Air Marshal Inamdar, and asked him for help. He said that his transport planes could fly the boats, if I could have the boats sent to the Bamrauli Airport. We directed the District Magistrate and Commissioner to requisition boats accordingly for the relief of Gorakhpur. They acted very fast. The boatmen in Allahabad were also very helpful. Soon the boats were transported on large transport aircrafts to Gorakhpur. It provided the necessary succour to the Gorakhpur administration. This is how the defence forces came to the aid of civil authority.

Immediately thereafter, the Prime Minister Sri Atal Bihari Vajpayee came to tour the flood affected areas. I was asked to give a PowerPoint presentation on Gorakhpur to the Prime Minister. I made extensive preparations and put it up to the Prime Minister. I was able to answer all the queries. Sri Kalyan Singh was extremely pleased. Central relief come soon thereafter.

Some months later there was a cloudburst in Uttarkashi. I was informed at 2.30 AM in the night by Sri Naresh Dayal, our Home Secretary that the entire district of Uttarkashi had been adversely affected and there was large scale destruction of houses and shops. I asked him to contact the Joint Secretary (Air) of the Defence Ministry in Delhi and request for an aerial survey of the district. This worked. By 4 AM the first sortie of the Air Force had taken off from Saharanpur. I telephoned the Chief Minister at 5 AM in the morning and apprised him of the damage caused. He wanted to immediately rush to Uttarkashi. I persuaded him not to do so as it would affect the relief work.

Balraj Vohra was the Divisional Commissioner of Garhwal. He was informing me of the steps he was taking and the requirement of asbestos sheets to rebuild the houses. I kept the Chief Minister informed. But one day, he decided to make an on-the-spot visit. Vohra rang me up to ask whether he should stay back to receive the Chief Minister or should he go ahead with going down to the plains for procuring supplies for the reconstruction of houses. I told him that he should concentrate on relief work and we would apprise the Chief Minister accordingly. Vohra rang up Naresh Dayal, the Home Secretary as well as Anurag Goel, Secretary to the Chief Minister and got the same advice.

However, the Chief Minister left early morning and none of us could inform him. When he landed at the District Headquarters he did not find the Commissioner and got extremely annoyed. When he came back to Lucknow in the afternoon there was a Cabinet Meeting. He refused to start the Cabinet Meeting till Vohra was suspended. Whenever the Home Secretary or I rose to speak he just refused to hear us. Kalyan Singh directed me to first issue the suspension order and only then would the Cabinet Meeting start. I was in a dilemma. Seeing the Chief Minister's adamant attitude, I called the Appointment Secretary and asked him to draft the suspension order and bring it to the Cabinet Room for my signature. Only when I had signed the order, the Chief Minister started the Cabinet meeting. While signing the order I quietly told Pradeep Shukla, the Appointment Secretary, not to issue the order till he hears from me. After all I had only been ordered to sign the suspension order which I had dutifully done.

In the afternoon, Kalyan Singh announced in the Assembly that he had ordered the suspension of the Commissioner of

Garhwal Division. Balraj Vohra rang me up asking whether the news was correct. Naresh Dayal and I felt guilty as he was being suspended for following our advice. I asked Vohra whether he had received any suspension order. He said, "no." I told him that we are trying to sort out the matter and advised him to come to Lucknow immediately. That same evening, Naresh Dayal and I got together and wrote a long note to the Chief Minister. We explained the situation to him and asked him to revoke the suspension order as the Commissioner had acted on our advice. If Vohra was guilty, so were we.

We asked for time to meet the Chief Minister. He was initially reluctant to do so. However, later he relented and gave an appointment. At the appointed time we went to the Chief Minister's room. We gave him our note and requested him to read it as we stood quietly. He read the note slowly and then without any further query, he approved our proposal for revocation of the suspension order. We thanked him and quietly walked out.

This was the greatness of Kalyan Singh. He had absolute trust in his Chief Secretary and in spite of announcing the suspension order in the Assembly, revoked it on our request. I began admiring him more and more.

On the announcement of the 5th Pay Commission recommendations, there was a demand that we, in the State, should also adopt the recommendations. A committee of Secretaries was set up to suggest the pay scales for State government employees. Based on the recommendations of this Committee, the government announced revision of pay scales in the State. But where were the finances to come from? Within three months, complaints began being received from separate treasuries of shortage of funds. Salaries not being paid. We kept on requesting the Central Government for increasing the overdrafts but we knew it could not continue for long.

I had a very good Secretary, Finance, Sushil Tripathi. A person with outstanding academic and administrative record, he suggested that we should approach the World Bank for a restructuring loan. After taking approval of the Chief Minister, we took up the matter with World Bank. A number of meetings were held with the officers of the World Bank who scrutinized all our accounts and other documents. Finally, after almost twelve months they prepared a loan agreement for discussion. We were asked to come to the USA to wrap up the loan agreement. Fortunately we had CM Vasudev as Secretary, Economic Affairs in the Government of India. He supported our initiative and sent his officer to USA to participate in the negotiations. We clinched the deal and were sanctioned ₹ 1,100 crore by the World Bank as part of the restructuring. This was the first restructuring loan for a State in India. Sri Kalyan Singh was extremely happy. Our State's budgeting problems got resolved.

As a postscript I must add that during the negotiations, I asked Sushil, whether we could have some conditions included, relating to reduction of staff in the State Government. I knew that if it came as part of the agreement the State Government would have to follow the condition in letter and spirit. He readily agreed and proposed some additional conditions which would force the State Government to give more funds to education and health. So, on our suggestions, many conditions were included in the loan agreement which were good for the financial condition of the State, but which would, in the normal course, never be accepted by our political masters.

The World Bank wanted the State legislature to also approve the loan agreement. We got these papers included in the papers circulated by the Assembly Secretariat to all the MLAs and reported compliance to the World Bank! Such papers are rarely read by the majority of the legislators.

Once we were travelling in the State plane together with the Finance Minister and the Chief Minister. As new ideas for the Budget were being discussed, first priority I suggested that like the Central Government, we should also impose a State cess on petrol, which would help raise resource for the maintenance of roads. It was readily agreed upon. Based on my experience of the road sector, I recommended that we should give more funds for construction of new highways as infrastructure always precedes development. This was immediately implemented in the State Budget for that year.

On the day preceding the Budget presentation, I was sitting with the Chief Minister and the Finance Secretary, reviewing para by para the entire speech. I sought the permission of the Chief Minister to amend the speech by adding one more paragraph. He looked at me. I told him that, based on my experience in the rural areas, we should amend the Zamindari Abolition Act and the Land Revenue Act to give the widow of the deceased farmer the same priority as the son. I informed him that the widows are treated very badly and if her name was included together with the son, in line of succession for the land holdings of the deceased, she would be treated with great respect. Sri Kalyan Singh liked the suggestion and immediately included it in his speech. This amendment was carried out and, I believe, it has brought immense relief to the widows.

In 2000, the Central Government decided to create a separate State of Uttaranchal. A draft Bill was sent to the State by the Centre, requesting for comments. We had a separate Department for Hill Development, under a Minister, Sri Ramesh Pokhriyal. Normally the Hill Development Department would have processed the Bill, but in this case, to enable an unbiased view, the Chief Minister asked the Chief Secretary to put up the Cabinet Note for consideration of the Cabinet.

Accordingly, I set up separate committees for distribution of assets, including irrigation and power, the training institutes, financial resources, agriculture institutes, stores, educational institutions, etc. Based on the recommendations of these committees, I put up a note before the Cabinet. The discussions went on the entire day and whatever decisions were taken, were incorporated in a note to the Chief Minister. These were then sent to the Central Government as representing the views of the State Government. One of the important suggestions made by Uttar Pradesh was that Haridwar should remain with Uttar Pradesh and the Ganga Canal headwork in Haridwar should be jointly controlled both by Uttar Pradesh and Uttaranchal.

The Central Government considered our views, but differed in a number of aspects, including the retention of Haridwar.

Some months later we were asked to propose the principles on which the officers of the All India Services as well as State civil services should be divided between the two States. Since there was no unanimity, a Committee was set up at the Central Government level under Sri UC Agarwal, former Secretary Personnel, to finalise the allocation. It was a mammoth exercise which included representations from hundreds of officers, who were affected. Some went to court, and I believe cases are still pending.

The Partition of assets and officers reminded me of the Partition effected by the British in 1947. I admired the way assets had at that time been divided between the two nations and the tremendous role, the civil services would have played in ensuring peaceful distribution of these assets. We were now playing the same role, but of course, without any animosity or rancour.

The Shia-Sunni problem had plagued Lucknow for over a hundred years. When I was District Magistrate of Lucknow, we had banned all processions as they had always led to violence and deaths. On returning to Lucknow as Chief Secretary after almost eighteen years, I found that the government was keen to ensure an amicable solution to the problem.

Both the sects had learnt to live peacefully over the years but it was an uneasy peace which occasionally also gave way to violence. Rajiv Rattan Shah, our Home Secretary was an extremely competent and energetic officer and had initiated a dialogue between the two communities. The Shias had finally agreed to allow the Sunnis one procession in a year as part of the proposed agreement. Shias in turn, with the approval of the Sunnis, were allowed to resume a limited number of processions. The District Magistrate, Lucknow, Sanjay Agarwal was the key negotiator. We apprised the Chief Minister of the progress and it was decided to take the risk of allowing these processions on both sides.

The Sunnis were happy that the one procession, they had been demanding for a long time, was being finally allowed. On the day, their procession wound its way in the streets of Lucknow, we sat glued to our seats. We kept ourselves abreast of the progress of the Sunni procession from locality to locality. There was a strong police *bandobast*. The District Magistrate was keeping an eye on all the developments. By afternoon the entire procession had passed off peacefully. We were relieved. The Chief Minister congratulated me, Home Secretary Rajeev Shah, the District Magistrate and SSP of Lucknow. It was indeed a historical initiative.

The Central Government was pressing the State Government to carry out reforms in the power sector. One of the major recommendations was the unbundling of the Electricity Board into separate Generation, Transmission and Distribution corporations. The Power Minister in Uttar

Pradesh was Sri Naresh Agarwal. He was very keen on the reforms and convinced the Chief Minister also. We were equally in support of the reforms as the power situation was getting worse everyday. The Power Engineers were opposed to the reforms and started an agitation. The Central Government was persuading us to speed up these reforms and promised all support. The entire State machinery was galvanized to counter the agitation by the power engineers. Reports of sabotage and deliberate disruption of power were pouring in. The District Magistrates were asked to take the help of local technicians and private sector engineers to counter the agitation. Eventually the reforms were carried out and separate corporations were carved out for generation, transmission and distribution. The Engineers withdrew their agitation after meeting the Power Minister Sri Naresh Agarwal. The Uttar Pradesh State Regulatory Authority in the Power sector was also set up with Sri JL Bajaj as the first Chairman.

Political opposition was, in the meantime, rising against Sri Kalyan Singh within the BJP. There was a great tussle between Sri Lalji Tandon and Sri Kalyan Singh. Sri Atal Bihari Vajpayee, the Prime Minister was supporting Sri Lalji Tandon. Finally, Sri Kalyan Singh was asked to resign and Sri Ram Prakash Gupta, was brought in as Chief Minister. He was a very simple person and depended a lot on the officers. There was no occasion when any disagreement arose between him and myself except on one occasion. As part of the reforms in the power sector, the World Bank had included metering by electronic meters in every household. Accordingly, as per World Bank regulations, international bidding was resorted to. In the bids received, the Chinese bid was technically and economically the best. When I sent the file for approval, the Chief Minister said that he would not give this order to the Chinese! It took two or three days for me and Sushil Tripathi, our Finance Secretary, to convince him that once we had accepted the World Bank loan for reforms in the power sector, then accordingly we will have to accept international bidding and the giving of the contract to the internationally best bidder. Sri Ram Prakash Gupta felt that the order should be given to anybody else, except the Chinese, whom he felt, were enemies of the nation! Finally he approved the proposal.

Sri Ram Prakash Gupta could not face up to the arm twisting by his colleagues also. Once it so happened that on the request of Sri Lalji Tandon, Minister for Urban Development, a certain police officer was posted as SSP, Lucknow. However, after two months Sri Lalji Tandon wanted to remove the officer. I told the Chief Minister that it would be very demoralizing for the officer to be removed so soon. The Chief Minister agreed. After two days, the Chief Minister called me and stated that Lalji Tandon had again pressed him to change the officer. I knew Lalji Tandon very well since I was District Magistrate of Lucknow. He was an excellent minister and always accepted whatever was rational. I told the Chief Minister that if we had to change the SSP I would like him to be posted as SSP, Kanpur an equally important charge. The Chief Minister said that he was not very sure whether Lalji Tandon would approve of this. I volunteered to talk to Sri Lalji Tandon. He agreed. I went and talked to Sri Lalji Tandon. Tandonji stated that he only wanted the officer to be removed from Lucknow and he would not mind if the officer was sent to the senior charge of Kanpur. Thus, the matter was amicably settled.

CHAPTER 8

Civil Defence Relations: Thoughts Before Leaving Lucknow to Join as Defence Secretary

THE telephone rang in the Chief Secretary's office in Lucknow. I was busy doing my files. The Information Officer, Srivastava was on the line. "Sir, have you read the news in *The Indian Express* today?"

"No", I said.

"Sir, you have been appointed as the Defence Secretary in the Government of India," he said.

I got a shock. For some time, I had been keen to go to the Centre on any post. I had completed two and a half years as Chief Secretary to the Government of Uttar Pradesh and was now keen to get back to Delhi.

As Chief Secretary I had certainly enjoyed my innings. To be number one in your own State is the ultimate joy of a civil servant. I had travelled extensively; encouraged new initiatives in each sector; took action against the corrupt; ensured decentralization of powers in terms of the 73rd and 74th amendment to the Constitution; reformed the entire power sector with the help of the Central Government and the World Bank; encouraged a strong NGO movement to help check on the executive at the ground level. The Chief Minister Sri Kalyan Singh had supported me thoroughly and when he was replaced by Sri Ram Prakash Gupta, the new Chief Minister also gave me the same confidence and trust. It was a smooth sailing for me in the last two and a half years in the State.

But mentally I was feeling restless. A feeling of satiation and ennui was slowly creeping in. I knew that I could continue as Chief Secretary for as long a period as I liked. There was no murmur amongst the ministers or the local politicians against me. I had excellent, forward-looking colleagues in the department of Home, Finance, Agriculture and Industries who were doing outstanding work and were a great support to me. All-in-all government was running smoothly but the feeling was also growing within me that my real work lay with the Central Government.

I had earlier made several requests to the Cabinet Secretary for my shifting to any Ministry in the Centre. But the Cabinet Secretary always consoled me by saying that the Chief Minister was so happy with me and that he will never agree to me being shifted to the Centre. I used to remind Cabinet Secretary every month of my request for posting to Delhi.

Therefore, when this news item appeared in *The Indian Express*, that I had been selected to be the next Defence Secretary, I was indeed very happy and grateful to the Cabinet Secretary for acceding to my request. I immediately telephoned the Cabinet Secretary, Sri Prabhat Kumar. The Cabinet Secretary was surprised at this news item and stated that no such decision has yet been taken. I was disappointed at the reply.

Next day I received a telephone call from the General Officer Commanding-in-Chief, Central Command, Lucknow, General Sarna, asking me whether I was moving to the Central Government as the Defence Secretary.

Apparently, his colleagues at the Army Headquarters rang him up from Delhi to ascertain the veracity of the newspaper report. I informed General Sarna that I had not received any such order as yet and I myself was trying to ascertain the actual facts.

I had excellent relations with General Sarna and his officers. Apart from the annual Civil-Military liaison conferences in which we sorted out the issues pending between the Defence establishments and the State Government, we were also interacting socially. My wife and his wife were extremely friendly. As the wife of the Chief Secretary, my wife headed the organization called 'AKANKSHA' whose membership included the wives of all IAS officers. On the other hand the wife of General Sarna was the head of the Army Wives Welfare Association, which included the wives of all the officers of the army posted in the Central Command. We used to meet quite frequently in the Mahomed Bagh Club in Lucknow which has membership both from the civilian as well as the defence officers. I used to make it a point to invite General Sarna and his Chief-of-Staff to all major civilian functions and General Sarna would do so in the army functions.

The necessity of maintaining friendly relations between the civil and military officers had been ingrained in us right from the beginning. Sometimes we needed their help and often they needed help from us. I could not forget that in 1999, when heavy floods inundated and blocked all approaches to Gorakhpur and some of the remaining districts in eastern

Uttar Pradesh, it was the Air Force Station at Allahabad, under Air Marshal Inamdar, which came to our rescue. An extremely amiable officer, Air Marshal Inamdar was a professional to the core. On a simple request made on telephone he had got his air transport planes to air lift more than 100 boats to the marooned districts. Air dropping of supplies was also arranged promptly. Air Marshal Inamdar was always in a jovial mood even as he went about his work professionally. Similarly, when there was an earthquake in Uttaranchal, and a telephone request was made by our Home Secretary at 2.30 AM in the morning, Air Force planes had soared in the sky within hours and were surveying the entire hilly areas without any delay.

The defence forces are extremely helpful when such a calamity occurs. On the other hand the defence forces also expect the civil administration, specially the district administration, to be sympathetic to the problem of ex-servicemen as well as the personnel who are serving on the front.

There are numerous problems faced by the servicemen when they have to leave their families behind while serving on the border. Sometimes their lands in the village are forcibly taken away or encroached by powerful people. The police does not always act in time to save the families of ex-servicemen from harassment by anti-social elements. There is nobody to look after their children. Though we have a Soldiers Board in each district, the Boards have become lethargic and bureaucratic. The District Magistrate is the ex-officio President of the District Soldiers' Board, but he hardly finds any time to go and attend the meetings. The officer-in-charge of the Soldiers Board is usually an ADM/SDM who looks after the working of the Soldiers' Board in addition to his own duties. The Secretary of the Board, who is usually an ex-serviceman, is the key figure and depending on his enthusiasm for the job, depends the working of the Board. However, the fact remains that servicemen, including ex-servicemen need tremendous help from the civil administration.

Jawans, who are recruited in the army, usually serve for 16 years unless they are promoted. After retirement they go back to their villages for settling down. In their long absence, several problems accumulate including encroachments on their plots, for which they need the help of district administration. Jawans are also put off by the corruption in the Revenue Administration and they face a lot of harassment from the Lekhpal/Patwari who keeps all the record of landholdings in the village. The period of leave sanctioned to the jawans is very restricted and they have to ensure that the Revenue Administration sorts out their problems within the limited period of their leave. If the matter is in the court, they have to waste a whole day in the court and away from their beloved ones whom they have come to see. This affects their morale when they are on the borders and this is not good for the nation. A separate cell should be set up in the office of the District Magistrate for settling the grievances of the servicemen as well as the ex-servicemen. The district officers must also visit some of the families of the servicemen and find out what problems they face. Servicemen, including ex-servicemen, should also be given priority when they go to meet the district administration officials.

Another problem which ex-servicemen face is employment after retirement. Jawans, as mentioned, retire early and the officers who do not make it to the top also retire early. While there is a full-fledged Resettlement Organization in the Defence Ministry and there is also a Directorate of Resettlement, the real problem lies in the field. These ex-servicemen have to be given priority in jobs where their qualification can meet the job requirements. This policy should not only be in the government sector but also in the private sector. The Corporates must give ex-servicemen preference over others in appointments.

When I was in the Defence Ministry I often used to wonder why we do not have Statutory Reservations for them. We are giving job reservations to Scheduled Caste/Scheduled Tribe/ Backward Classes based on caste. Why not give 10% reservations within these vertical reservations. This would be a big morale booster for the servicemen, especially the jawans. Age restrictions must also be relaxed for them. It may perhaps make the services more attractive to the youth of our country.

As Chief Secretary of the State, I was also one of the two rotating Chairmen of the Mahomed Bagh Club, Lucknow. We each had a tenure of one year. The other Chairman in the alternative years was the Chief-of-Staff of the GOC-in-C, Central Command. My officers used to often tell me that, based on protocol, I was at par with the GOC-in-C Central Command. This protocol of equivalence between the civil officers and the military officers has always been a subject of heated discussions in the higher echelon of both the services. In the district it is well-accepted that the District Magistrate is equivalent to a Brigadier. The Divisional Commissioner in protocol is equivalent to Major-General. It is not clear thereafter as to what is the equivalence between the Secretaries in the State/Chief Secretary of a State and the defence officers. While the Chief Secretary in the State has the same scale as the Defence Secretary in the Centre and therefore, is equivalent to the GOC-in-C and Vice-Chief of Staff, but the Secretaries in the State get pay scale of Additional Secretary in the Government of India and should be equivalent to the those

Lieutenant-Generals who are not of the level of GOC-in-C/ Vice-Chief of Army/Air Force/Navy.

The issue of equivalence between the army officers and civilian officers led to a very interesting matter. When I was Principal Secretary to the Governor, Uttar Pradesh in 1994 a proposal was received in the Governor's office from the Mahomed Bagh Club, that the Governor may agree to become Patron of the Mahomed Bagh Club. The then Chief Secretary of Uttar Pradesh, TSR Subramaniam got to know about it and came to see me and advised me to request the Governor not to accept this proposal. The Chief Secretary pointed out that GOC-in-C Central Command was already the Patron of the club and making the Governor as Patron, would appear to make the Governor equivalent to the GOC-in-C in protocol. This would disturb the entire protocol as the GOC-in-C would look upon the Chief Secretary as an officer lower in rank (as Chief Secretary works under the Governor). Needless to say that the Governor was promptly informed of the implication of the proposal and understanding the mischief behind it, he politely declined the offer. Such games are always played between the civilian and military officers.

After being given a warm farewell by the entire cabinet of Uttar Pradesh, which passed a resolution commending my services to the State. I started making preparations for joining the coveted post of the Defence Secretary of India. The order from the Central Government had been formally received by the State Government and though the Chief Minister, late Sri Ram Prakash Gupta, requested me to stay back as Chief Secretary, I politely told him that this would not be possible as I was keen to work in the Centre.

I was given a farewell party by the officers of the Central Command in Lucknow. General Sarna and his wife had been extremely kind and affectionate to both of us. General Sarna had already informed me that he was also getting transferred to the Western Command at Chandi Mandir in Chandigarh. We had already organized a farewell for him and his wife on behalf of the State Government. The farewell dinner was arranged in the Civil Services Officers Institute and was attended by all the senior secretaries of the Government of Uttar Pradesh. The relations between army and the civil administration had never been too cordial as they were at that time.

As news of my departure spread, spate of farewell parties followed. I had the unique distinction of being towed together with my wife sitting in the car, by the senior officers of the State Government. The enthusiastic officers had brought a long rope which they tied to my car and pulled it for some distance. I had heard such a farewell being given in the defence forces but never on the civilian side. Both my wife and I were extremely moved by this affection.

As we reached the Railway Station and moved toward my coach I found it decorated with flowers and a huge crowd of officers as well as public waiting for me. Tons and tons of garlands of flowers were put on the neck of my wife and myself. Both my wife and I stood in front of the coach. The crowd kept on increasing. There were several sports organizations I had patronized and their representatives were there; the dramatic and art organizations which I had encouraged, were also there. NGOs who had given their services to the administration, on my request, were also present. The poor people I had helped from time to time were also there. Several retired officers were present.

Suddenly I found my senior colleague, late AP Singh rushing with a garland, five minutes before the train was to leave. AP Singh was a dear friend always full of life and humour. I can never forget him.

The crowd on the platform was swelling every minute.

I think it must have been a relief to the Railway authorities when the train finally chugged off platform number 1 of the Char Bagh Railway Station of Lucknow.

On 20th October we landed at the New Delhi Railway station. I immediately proceeded to Uttar Pradesh Bhawan to freshen myself. When I rang up TR Prasad, Defence Secretary, he advised me to come in a white 'Bund Gala' (closed collar) suit. I was surprised and asked him why. Prasad stated that at 11 o'clock, that very day an investiture ceremony was to take place at the Rashtrapati Bhawan and since I was taking over charge in the morning I should conduct the ceremonies in his place. I was aghast and taken aback. But to say no to the incumbent Cabinet Secretary was out of question. So, I braced myself, went to the Defence Ministry and proceeded straight to Rashtrapati Bhawan, thereafter. I had wanted to formally call on the Defence Minister Sri George Fernandez, before taking charge, but learnt that he had already proceeded to Rashtrapati Bhawan to brief the President about the ceremony.

On reaching Rashtrapati Bhawan, I saw Sri George Fernandez. He was very happy to see me and enquired whether I had taken charge. I said I had done so and also informed him that I would be conducting the investiture ceremony in place of TR Prasad. I was advised of the procedure and protocol of the ceremony which included requesting the Hon'ble President for permission to start the above proceedings in the beginning and then requesting for closure at the end of the proceedings. I was given my two line dialogue in writing which I kept in my hand just in case I forgot.

At exactly 11 o'clock I smartly walked towards the President and clicked my shoes when I turned to face him. He was obviously surprised to see me, as he was not informed of the change of guard in the Defence Ministry. I read out my dialogue, requesting his permission to start the proceedings (it seemed so much like the old days when the King's permission had to be taken before starting any proceedings in his presence). Permission being given I went smartly back to my seat. I say 'smartly' because several senior Lieutenant-Generals and other officers who came and introduced themselves later, complimented me on the 'smart steps' and the 'right turn' saying that probably it was better than what a number of defence officers could have done. I also met a number of senior civilian officers as well as ministers present at the function. I was grateful to TR Prasad for having given me a chance to conduct the investiture proceedings as it gave me a chance to meet several defence officers and other personalities.

I had finally arrived in the fraternity which I was expected to lead wisely and responsibly for the next two years, till I retired.

The Defence Secretary's office is awe inspiring, as the location is on Rajpath. It overlooks the Rajpath and commands a magnificent view right up to India Gate. Housed in what is called South Block, it is part of the complex which includes the Ministry of External Affairs as well as the Prime Minister's Office. On the opposite side, the complex is called 'North Block' which houses the Home Ministry, Finance Ministry and the Department of Personnel and Training. These offices taken together, both in the South Block and the North Block, constitute the core offices of the Government of India and all those who sit in these offices feel they are a part of the 'Elite'. The Defence Ministry is located on the eastern part of the South Block. While the Defence Secretary's office is located on the Janpath end, the Defence Minister's office is located on the opposite end. This has been traditionally so for a number of years. While no attempt has ever been made to shift the Defence Secretary from his room an attempt was made in 2001 to do so. But more of it later.

The Defence Secretary also has a very clear view of the Parliament building, which highlights the majestic splendour of democracy through its architecture. It has an outstanding structure made of stone and has a similar use of stone, as the structures of the North Block and the South Block. One wonders whether the British ever imagined that the building would one day house the Indian Parliament. Delhi was declared the capital of India in 1911. But nowhere were the elected legislatures functioning democratically, as full democracy had not yet been accepted by the Britishers as an intrinsic policy of the colonial rule. The foundation stone of the Parliament House or the Council House, as it was originally known, was laid on 12th February 1921 by the Duke of Connaught. The opening ceremony of the Parliament House was performed on 18th January 1927 by the then Governor-General of India Lord Irwin. Prior to this, the Central Assembly and the Legislative Council (predecessor of the Central Assembly) used to meet at the Old Secretariat, Delhi. Prior to this, till 1911, it used to meet at Kolkata (Calcutta). Construction of the building was done under the supervision of two famous architects – Sir Edwin Lutyens (1869-1944) and Sir Herbert Baker (1862-1946). At that time the total construction cost had come to ₹ 83 lakh (8.3 million). The building originally housed the Legislative Council, the Chamber of Princes and the Library. Today it houses the Rajya Sabha (Council of States), the Lok Sabha (House of the People) as well as the offices of the Chairman, Deputy Chairman, Rajya Sabha, Speaker, Deputy Speaker, Lok Sabha,

Ministers, Chairmen of Parliamentary Committees, offices of the political parties, groups recognized by the Speaker for this purpose as well as the Ministry of Parliamentary Affairs. Both the Secretary-Generals of the Rajya Sabha and the Lok Sabha sit here, as well as Secretary, Parliamentary Affairs, Branches of the Secretariat of both the Houses are also located here as well as several committees.

The Central Hall, located at the centre of the building, is usually a crowded place as, old and new members of Parliament, MLAs, former ministers and the accredited press representatives mingle with each other. This is the hall where the Constituent Assembly had met and had adopted the Constitution in 1950.

Coming back to the Defence Secretary's office, the complex, if it may be so-called, consists of a room for the Staff Officer of the Defence Secretary, a separate Conference Hall, and a spacious well laid out space inside the Defence Secretary's office where he can hold his meetings. On the left side of the office of Defence Secretary, are wooden shelves, stacked with files and books. One of the most coveted books in Defence Secretary is the Henderson Brooke Report which is kept under lock and key. It cannot be taken out of the Defence Secretary's room and cannot be given or lent out to any person, including the ministers. I must confess that I have not seen the relevant Order but these instructions are orally passed on from one Defence Secretary to another.

As one walks down the corridor from the Defence Secretary's room, one will first go past the room of the Chief of Army Staff and then the room of the Chief of Naval Staff. The Air Chief's office is not located in this building but it is located in Vayu Bhawan, the building located near the roundabout, very close to and opposite to Udyog Bhawan.

There is also a closely guard operation room located in the Defence Ministry where often the Army holds its briefing for the Prime Minister and/or the Defence Minister and other specially invited officers like Secretary, Ministry of External Affairs, Cabinet Secretary, etc.

In the same complex is the office of the Secretary, Defence Production as well as that of the Secretary, Defence Research and Development. However, later a separate demarcated area outside the Ministry was allocated for the Defence Research and Development Organization (DRDO), and today a beautiful complex of the DRDO has come up on the Southern side of the Defence Ministry building.

Several defence organizations were allotted defence land for housing their offices in the twenty months that I was there. One was the IDSA (Institute of Defence Studies and Analysis). The second one was the Directorate of Defence Estates which has come up near the Palam (Domestic) Airport. Yet another was for the office of BrahMos, a joint venture between Russia and India to produce the fastest and most accurate guided missiles.

There is also a separate section in the Defence Ministry dealing with War History. It is not a very active branch and has little work to do. However, there has been demand from time to time to activate this branch. Official histories of the Kargil war, 1971 Indo-Pak war and the 1965 Indo-Pak war are yet to be written.

Relationship and Coordination with the Ministry of External Affairs

The Ministry of Defence works very closely with the Ministry of External Affairs in its relations with foreign countries. All the visits of the Defence Chiefs as well as the Defence Secretary to various countries is coordinated with the help and advice from the Ministry of External Affairs. In the weekly meetings which the Defence Minister holds, apart from the Defence Secretary and other Secretaries of the Ministry of Defence who are present, the two special invitees are the Secretary, Ministry of External Affairs and the Cabinet Secretary.

In these weekly meetings all the Chiefs – Army, Air Force and Navy – are present. All common issues as well as pending matters are discussed. Any proposal pending with Defence Ministry received from the Chiefs or vice-versa are brought forward, discussed and resolved before the next meeting. Kashmir was a perennial topic on the agenda with the Army Chiefs pointing out how many attempts have been made by the militants to sneak into Indian territory and how many militants were killed. The number of deaths of the security personnel, was also discussed. I remember during the January-May 2002 period the 'kill ratio' that is death of members of the security forces and the number of militants killed was causing us worry. The Army Chief emphasized on the purchase of night vision devices as well as bullet proof vests. He also emphasized on expeditious procurement of the same.

In the War Room whenever there was detailed discussion on the incursion by the Chinese, the Secretary of the Ministry of External Affairs was always present. Issues were raised, discussed and future steps finalized.

An officer of the Ministry of External Affair is always taken on deputation in the Ministry of Defence at the level of Joint Secretary. He is also in-charge of coordinating the training programmes of foreigners in the various defence institutes of India. Each year the Defence Ministry allots slots to various countries who would like their officers to be trained in the various Defence Training Institutes of India under the Defence Ministry. In my time we had a very fine officer of the Ministry of External Affairs, Bambit Roy heading the division.

The Ministry of External Affairs also coordinates all visits of the foreign dignitaries who would like to interact with the Defence Minister, the three Chiefs and the Defence Secretary or who want to visit Defence installations and Institutions. The programmes are drawn up by the Ministry of External Affairs in consultation with the concerned Chief, or the Defence Secretary. We were also briefed by the MEA on the issues likely to be raised and the replies to be given keeping in view the foreign policy and national interest. We also have several countries with whom we have standing arrangements of meeting every six month on defence related issues. The usual practice is that these meetings are held once in India and once in the other country by rotation. The agreements are drafted and signed either in the presence of the Defence Minister or if it is part of a bigger agenda, in the presence of the Prime Minister. Agreements are drafted beforehand leaving any tendentious clauses to be decided during the meeting.

During my time, in October 2001, the Indo-US defence group was restarted after a long gap. The USA had been boycotting all defence related talks with India since 1998 when we had our Pokhran blasts. Even the agreement we had reached in 1995 (prior to the nuclear bomb tests) on the supply by US of weapon locating radars, was not implemented. However, in 2001 we got an indication from MEA that the USA wanted to restart the talks. Meeting dates were finalized. The US defence delegation which came, was headed by the USA Under Secretary of Defence (equivalent to our Defence

Secretary) Douglas Feith. We had a very active US Ambassador in India. He was extremely keen for a close working defence relationship with India. He met me as well as the Defence Minister separately. We discussed matters of mutual interest. It is on this occasion that I also met for the first time the young distinguished defence analyst Ashley Tellis. Born in Mumbai he is an American citizen who has been an active member of the US Defence Think Tank establishment. Ashley had been specifically appointed to the US Embassy in India to aid and advise the US Ambassador on matters relating to defence. I found Ashley to be a good friend who genuinely had the interest of both India and USA in mind.

The visit by Douglas Feith, Under Secretary, Department of Defence, was an outstanding success. We signed a deal which not only saw a major breakthrough in defence relationships but also opened the US market for defence purchases by India. Soon after the agreement the Ministry decided to go in for the purchase of Weapons Locating Radars through the US Government. A delegation under the Additional Secretary, Defence Procurement, Sri Ajai Vikram Singh was finalized to proceed to Washington to finalize the deal.

Thereafter, one after another, several delegations came from the USA to discuss proposals for intelligence sharing, logistic cooperation and protection of US shipping through the Malacca Straits. In all these negotiations a representative of the MEA used to be always present to guide our deliberations.

After the attacks on Parliament by the terrorists in December 2001, while the defence forces were bracing themselves for 'Operation Parakram' on the border, the Defence Minister, myself and a team of officers went to USA to meet the Secretary for Defence, on the advice of MEA. But more of that later.

There are several countries with which India has defence cooperation agreements. Some are high powered meetings headed by the Defence Ministers of both the countries and some are alternatively chaired by the Defence Secretaries of India and the concerned country. Every delegation on our side always consists of the representatives of the three wings, ie Army, Air Force and Navy, the concerned Joint/Additional Secretary dealing with the subject matter of negotiations as well as a representative of MEA. The final drafting of the agreement is always couched in diplomatic language with a determination to meet again.

A very important issue in deciding on these delegation is equivalence. The heads of the delegations have to be of the same political or official status. If the status of one delegation is lower than the head of the other delegation, then changes are made accordingly. This is always based on the advice given by MEA.

I still remember a visit to Italy in June 2002. After the delegates had interacted and we had inspected the torpedo manufacturing unit, we set down to finalize the agreement. Our Ambassador in Italy insisted that the agreement should include a clause saying that the Italian Government supports us, on the Kashmir issue. He said that these instructions were sent to all the embassies by the MEA and this clause has to be included in the agreement. We discussed this issue with our Italian counterpart but they said that they had no brief for this and this clause cannot be included in the agreement. We kept on having the farewell dinner hosted by the Italian side for the delegates. Our Ambassador kept on telling me in Hindi, across the dinner table, not to sign the agreement. Our hosts kept on waiting for us to sign the agreement. This was embarrassing for all of us. I felt it was unfair to insist on this clause on Kashmir as part of our agreement. We had also not been briefed on this aspect in India. I then decided to sign the agreement without the Kashmir clause. We finally left at 12 o'clock in the night. Our hosts were relieved. Our Ambassador was very unhappy with my decision but he knew that as the head of the delegation it was I, who had to take the final decision and I had decided. This issue was never raised by MEA when I came back to India and it left me with an impression that our Ambassador in Italy was briefing me incorrectly.

Another interesting incident happened in Moscow when we went with our Defence Minister Sri Jaswant Singh. The discussions were to take place in the Kremlin and President Putin was to lead the Russian delegation. Our Ambassador in Moscow, Sri Raghunathan had informed us that security was very tight in the Kremlin. We were all given authenticated identity cards for entry to the Kremlin. When we reached there with Sri Jaswant Singh, our Defence Minister, we found that he had been stopped by the guards at the Kremlin. Sri Jaswant Singh had forgotten to bring his authenticated identity card and the guard would not let him in. Sri Jaswant Singh had been a Major in the Army and he felt highly insulted. "I can't be stopped by a subaltern," he stated and decided that the entire delegation should go back in protest. Our Ambassador tried his best to argue with the guard but the guard had clear instructions not to allow any one without an identity card. Raghunathan then intentionally raised his voice, so that the senior officers of the Kremlin could hear him. It worked. They promptly came running. Our Ambassador explained the situation to them and informed them that the meeting was with President Putin and any delay would neither be tolerated by him nor by us. The senior officer understood and while advising us that the minister should have brought the card issued to him, allowed us entry. Thereafter, the meeting proceeded smoothly. These hiccups often occur, but we leave it to our Ambassadors to smoothen the issues.

Yet another interesting incident took place when our Defence Minister Sri George Fernandez was leading a delegation for defence talks with the USA in Washington in the second week of January 2002. As I went through the security check, the burly black American official discovered a bottle of hair oil in my hand bag. He asked me what it was and I replied that it was hair oil. He looked at me disbelievingly. I then opened the bottle, took out a bit of the hair oil and put it on my head. He then allowed me in.

Then I noticed that George Fernandez was also being vigorously frisked. In the VIP culture I had grown up in India, we had never seen the sight of a minister being vigorously frisked. After the frisking, George Fernandez was asked to take off his shoes and searched again. We felt it highly insulting and demeaning. In my mind I wondered how the Americans would take it if their Secretary of State was frisked and asked to take off his shoes for a security check. I made up my mind to recommend this 'tit for tat' strategy when I came back to India. But we never retaliated. The only country that retaliated in the same manner was Brazil which till date, I am told, insists on frisking the American dignitaries when they visit Brazil.

Despite these incidents, I must state that I grew up admiring the professional staff of our Embassies and the members of the Indian Foreign Service. They are performing tough jobs, far away from home. Every minister, junior or senior, expects the Ambassador to personally receive him, which is impossible, keeping in mind the multiplicity of activities which our Ambassadors have to perform. In several

Embassies I also noticed that they have outsourced this function of receiving and seeing off VIPs to people, whom they take on contract, for these duties only, as they are unable to spare the regular staff/officers for this purpose.

Relationship with the Three Chiefs

The Defence Secretary is lower in salary and protocol vis-a-vis the Chiefs of the Army, Navy and the Air Force. While three Chiefs get the salary of the Cabinet Secretary, the Defence Secretary get the salary which any other Secretary to the Government of India gets. Even in the Warrant of Precedence while the three Chiefs are in the same standing as the Cabinet Secretary, the Defence Secretary is placed in Article 24, ie in the category allotted to Secretaries. Depending upon the date when he joined as Secretary, he is allotted a seat in the enclosure provided for Secretaries.

All the GOCs of the Indian Army, as well as the Vice-Chief and the Lieutenant-General in-charge of the Training Command in the Army get the same pay scale as a Secretary to the Government of India. Similar is the position in the Air Force and the Navy. The Defence Secretary's meetings are usually attended by the Vice-Chiefs and the Defence Secretary presides as *primus inter pares* (first amongst equals). This is also true of the Defence Secretary vis-a-vis the other Secretaries of the Ministry of Defence. It is the Defence Secretary who coordinates all policy matters within the Ministry.

The formal protocol position of the Defence Secretary vis-a-vis the Defence Chiefs notwithstanding, the Defence Chiefs are very respectful of the Defence Secretary. Often they would just walk into my room for a chat without any structured agenda. I remember once General Padmanabhan, Chief of Army Staff, walked into my room and insisted in sitting in the chair around my office table, instead of the sofa set. He said he felt quite comfortable in the office chair and further stated that it would also help me in or attending to the telephones (which were quite in number) on the telephone table. The Air Chief Marshal Tipnis and later Krishnamurthy and the Navy Chief Sushil Kumar and Malvender Singh also would to do the same. The Chiefs were the friendliest people I ever met, extremely polite and courteous. They had no airs and no feeling of superiority. While I treated them with all respect, they reciprocated in ample measure.

The Army Chief has his room down the corridor, not very far from the Defence Secretary's room. In my time, as the Army Chief was the senior most, the Committee of the Chiefs of Staff used to meet in the Army Chief's room. On some occasions when I wanted to discuss issues with all the Chiefs, I would walk into the Army Chief's room, simply giving prior intimation to him via the RAX telephone. This often avoided a lot of paper work and helped to expedite matters.

Attack on Parliament

In December 2001, there was a terrorist attack on Parliament. Sitting in my room in the Defence Ministry, I could hear the shots being fired. While I was trying to find out what was happening, my officers rushed in to inform me about the terrorist attack. The doors of the Ministry were immediately closed and guards took position round the building.

George Fernandez, our Defence Minister was inside Parliament. He rang up the local Military Commander who immediately galvanized his troops and started moving towards Parliament. The Delhi Police Commissioner Ajai Raj Sharma rushed to the spot while the local security guards inside Parliament fought the terrorists and eventually succeeded in neutralizing them. Several of our Parliament security personnel as well as secretariat staff also fell prey to the bullets.

There was shock and disbelief at this blatant attack. The government reacted swiftly. It was decided to have a massive build up of our troops on the border. The Railways were activised for the troop movements. The government was keen to take some covert action but were advised restraint by USA and other powers.

The meeting of the Cabinet Committee on Security was convened to chalk out action by land, sea and air against Pakistan. This was the famous 'Operation Parakram'.

The Cabinet Committee on Security was informed of the immediate requirements of arms and equipment by the Army and the Air Force. I was directed by the CCS to suggest a procedure for emergency purchases. We prepared a draft and then I took it to the Chiefs of Staff Committee for discussion. After due deliberations I was able to finalize a draft emergency procedure for procurement, and after getting approval of the Defence Minister I put it up to the CCS for approval. It was duly approved the next day and we were able send a team to USSR for emergency purchases.

The Army had put up some additional requirements of military equipments. Since it was urgently required I rang up my Israeli counterpart. Israel was more than ready to supply the equipment at previously negotiated rates. They sent a defence team next day. About half the items were supplied free of cost by the Israeli government. Israel is a true all weather friend of India.

Our troops were amassed on the border by the first week of January. USA advised us not to escalate the conflict and put pressure on Pakistan to come out with a conciliatory statement.

In the meantime communal riots had flared up in Gujarat. The Cabinet Secretary rang me up to say that troops may be required to be moved to Gujarat and we should be ready accordingly. I informed General Vij the Vice-Chief of Army to initiate preliminary preparations. The CCS met in the evening and approved the movement of troops to the State. Army units were moved from the border to Gujarat.

The Railways worked efficiently which enabled this movement speedily. However the time taken to move the troops to move to the border caused us concern.

The congeniality between the Defence Chiefs and the Defence Secretary depends upon the personal nature of each person. It is not subject to protocol formalities. Often as Defence Secretary I would go to Vayu Bhawan whenever a secret presentation was to be made or I would simply talk on telephone with the Chiefs.

One of the legacies I inherited when I became the Defence Secretary, were the files in which there was difference of opinion relating to personnel and disciplinary matters between the office of the Defence Secretary and the Army Chief. The differences were not personal but were a result of different opinions being put up in the two establishments and being dittoed as normal by the Defence Secretary and the Army Chief. This happens in many offices but becomes more acute as it is presented as a difference between the Defence Ministry and the Army Headquarters. There were thirteen cases in all. The files were put up to the Defence Minister and both the Army Chief and I were called for discussion. Both of us stated that the files represented the departmental point of view and that both of us were open to whatever decision the Defence Minister took. After about a week we got the files back wherein in some files the Defence Minister agreed with the views of the Army Chief and in some with the views of the Defence Ministry. We happily closed the files. In my entire tenure thereafter the Army Chief and I had no disciplinary related issues in which we differed. When the Army Chief reminded me of any pending issue I would get it promptly settled and vice-versa. General Padmanabhan was an extremely courteous and polite person with a unique sense of humour.

After having been in office for some months, I found that there were numerous occasions when the three Chiefs would host parties, whether it was the Commander's Conference, a farewell, Army Day, Navy Day, Air Force Day, etc. I felt that the Defence Secretary must also do so. I asked my Additional Secretary Ajay Prasad whether I could host a party for the Chiefs and other senior officers, and whether it would be treated as official expenditure. Ajai stated that there was no budget head for such parties to be thrown by the Defence Secretary. I asked as to how the three Chiefs did it. Ajai came back and said that in their case, the expenditure is borne from their regimental funds whereas the Defence Secretary had no such funds. I asked him to find out a solution. He came back the next day with a very simple solution.

Out of the profits of the Canteen Store Depots, annual distribution of funds is done for various activities of each wing of the Defence Forces. In the ensuing meeting of the CSD which was to be held under the Chairmanship of the Defence Minister, I proposed an allocation of ₹ 5 lakh to the Defence Secretary for hosting functions for the Defence Forces. As this was a meagre amount out of the total profits it was easily agreed to. Since then the Defence Secretary has been hosting parties on numerous occasions, including the Commanders Conferences, farewells to the Chiefs on their retirement, etc. It brought the Defence Secretary closer to the senior officers of the defence forces and the three Chiefs were very happy that the Defence Secretary was hosting parties during their Annual Conferences. It added colour and variety to such meets as the officers of the Defence forces could freely interact with the officers of the Ministry in a congenial atmosphere.

Soon after taking charge as Defence Secretary, I had gone to call on PK Kaul, former Defence Secretary who later rose to the position of Cabinet Secretary in the tenure of Smt Indira Gandhi as Prime Minister. I sought his advice on the running of the Defence Ministry. PK Kaul was a capable, astute and a practical civil servant. He said,

> "Yogendra, there are three things which I was unable to do as Defence Secretary and which you must endeavour to do. One is that the Defence Secretary must have an earmarked house, as the three Chiefs have. Second, you must have a flag for your car because in functions held by the Chiefs, the ordinary soldier or military policeman sees only whether it is a flag car or not. If it is flag here, he gives it due importance otherwise he will send your car for parking elsewhere. Thirdly you must also have funds to host parties for senior military and defence personnel like the three Chiefs. Such parties brings you closer to the officers and give a deeper understanding of what they feel and think."

I started working on these three suggestions. Till my time, the Defence Secretary had no earmarked house. In fact when I joined as Defence Secretary, I was treated like any other Secretary, and had to await the allotment of a house for myself. Before leaving the post of Chief Secretary, Uttar Pradesh, I had made a request to the Engineer-in-Chief Irrigation to temporarily allot the Irrigation Inspection House in Okhla to me till I got a regular house allotment from the Central

Government. This was a beautiful located guest house, near a pond, very close to the Holy Family Hospital. However, it was very far from the South Block office and therefore I was not connected by RAX, the secret telephone line connecting all government Secretaries and senior officers. During the six weeks I stayed there I used to get urgent messages of clashes on the Kashmir border but had to use the ordinary MTNL line to talk to the Hon'ble Defence Minister.

I requested the Defence Minister to write to Sri Jagmohan, Union Urban Development Minister (in-charge of government housing) to earmark a house for the Defence Secretary. I was very surprised when my minister received a reply promptly, stating that the Ministry of Urban Development agrees to the proposal and henceforth the house in which I was staying (11, Pandara Road) would be earmarked as the house of the Defence Secretary. I was quite surprised at this achievement. Later on my successor got another bigger house on Akbar Road earmarked for the Defence Secretary. This house is much better and compares favourably with the houses allotted to the Vice-Chiefs.

I next started working on designing a flag for the car of the Defence Secretary. This exercise was done in house and the file was presented to the Defence Minister in six weeks. Now this being an entirely new initiative, the Defence Minister was advised by his office to seek the views of the Cabinet Secretary. It turned out that the Cabinet Secretary also has no flag of his own and his car as well as the car of other Secretaries also do not have flags. The file therefore remained in cold storage and never returned from the Cabinet Secretariat.

The absence of a flag did lead to embarrassing situations. I remember that when the Naval Fleet was being reviewed by the President of India in Bombay in February 2001 I was also invited by the Naval Chief. Arrangements for accommodation were made in a separate building. My wife and I were housed in decent rooms but the car we were given was a small Fiat and naturally not fitted with any flag. Whenever we participated in an official function, while the Ambassador cars with flags carrying the Chief, Vice-Chiefs and other senior defence dignitaries were allowed to pass through, our car used to be stopped at very far off places and we had to walk our way through. The senior defence officers were of course were very apologetic and considerate and would offer to give me lifts in their cars. But the other problem was that if I travelled in their car, my allotted car and the staff officer of the Navy allotted to me would be lost. So, I would politely refuse their offer and continue to commute in my own small car allotted to me. The junior officers of the Navy, Air Force and Army are not very aware of the role and position of the Defence Secretary in their hierarchy. They are only aware of the hierarchy in their own defence set up. This is unlike other Ministries where Secretaries have their own importance as they also visit sites in the field and the junior officers recognize them through interactions at various levels. The Defence Secretary has his interaction at very high levels in the defence forces and it is only occasionally that he visits the troops in the border or on the front.

The interaction with the senior defence personnel depends entirely on one's own nature and personality. Except for the protocol equivalence with the Vice-Chief there is no other convention which governs this relationship. However at the senior levels there is utmost courtesy and politeness and a Defence Secretary usually feels at home with them. The wife of the Defence Secretary is also given the utmost courtesy and is invited to all the functions hosted by the wives of the Chiefs.

To reciprocate the dinners we used to have at the residence of the Chief, I decided to host a dinner at my residence in Pandara Road. I personally invited all the three Chiefs and the Vice-Chiefs, Brijesh Misra, Adviser to the Prime Minister and Adviser National Security Council, Secretary Defence Production, Secretary Personnel and some others. As there was no well laid-out protocol for the drill I sent a message to the local SHO that these high ranking VIPs were coming for dinner at my place. This I felt was necessary, for security reasons. The SHO was quite puzzled as to what is he expected to do as he had never been through such a drill before!

I checked up my liquor cupboard to ensure that there was no shortage. Glasses were cleaned up, soda bought in ample quantity together with ice. I and my wife had to personally supervise everything as there was no precedent and we did not have the domestic staff which had been trained to handle such situations.

I was grateful when everyone, I had invited, came. The Army Chief told me that he had made a programme for a visit to one of the field stations but he had cancelled the trip to be present. The dinner went off very well and everyone went back, in a happy mood. I was told later by one of the Chiefs, that, as they had never received such an invitation from any Defence Secretary before, they had discussed this together and decided that all of them must be present at this dinner. I do think it contributed to the bonhomie between all of us for the rest of my tenure.

Gujarat Earthquake

The Republic Day Parade on Rajpath is organized and managed by the Defence Ministry. The entire parade, including the selection of Jhankis, the performance of school children, the selection of cultural programmes, and the march past is controlled and directed by the Ministry of Defence and the three service headquarters. On 26th January 2002 as the magnificent and impressive parade concluded, news flowed in of the massive earthquake in Bhuj and other parts of Gujarat. Report of people dying, including the defence personnel posted in the earthquake affected areas, kept flowing throughout the day.

Relief operations started on a war footing. The Navy, Air Force and Army were alerted and all moved in their men and medical staff for the aid of the suffering population. The Navy moved its ships with personnel and material to the coastal areas of Gujarat. The Army men moved in with doctors and engineers to help those trapped under the debris.

The Beating Retreat ceremony was to take place as planned on the 29th January 2010. A big question arose as to whether, in the above circumstances, the ceremony should be held at all.

This ceremony had been taking place without break for the last five decades. As defence personnel and their families had also been affected and some had also died during the earthquake, requests for cancelling the Beating Retreat ceremony began emerging from the service headquarters. I rang up the Defence Minister Sri George Fernandez, who was amongst the first to reach Gujarat, to organize the massive relief operation and apprised him of the sentiments expressed here on the holding of the Beating Retreat ceremony. He readily agreed to cancel the Beating Retreat ceremony. Orders were issued accordingly and everybody was informed through the Press and TV of the cancellation.

We now concentrated on relief efforts. The army is usually the first to reach to the aid of civil authorities in such cases and they did so. A field hospital was established and doctors of the Army did a magnificent job in treating all the injured. The Navy and Air Force helped in rushing essential medical and food supplies to the affected regions.

The Air Force Station at Bhuj was badly affected with several injured people as well as some casualties. The Air Force carried out several sorties for transporting essential supplies to the affected population. Massive relief operations were mounted all over the country. Food supplies as well as clothes came pouring from all corners. Several people lay injured under the debris. There were no gas cutters which could cut through the cement concrete boundaries and rescue the survivors. The Army put out all its men and equipment for the relief efforts.

From this situation evolved the idea of setting up three or more disaster centres under the Army in various parts of the country. The Army was requested to identify the equipment required. Separate budget allocations were made for setting up such disaster centres. At present of course we have the National Disaster Management Authority under which all such centres of the defence forces as well as the State Governments get coordinated.

Aid to civil authorities has been one of the foremost functions of the defence forces. The civil authorities all over the country depend heavily on their equipments as well as on the personnel of the forces to support them at times of such disaster.

Relations Between the Defence Officers and the Civil Servants

The younger personnel of the defence forces are very critical of civilians in general and civil bureaucracy in particular. In social gatherings, where civilian and defence officials are together, the phrase 'damn civilians' is often heard. The reason for this is historical.

Initially in the seventeenth century, the British East India employed European enlisted personnel to guard the factories and trading posts set up in Surat and Bombay. By the eighteenth century the Presidencies had emerged and the locally employed personnel were organized on military lines. The three Presidencies – Bombay, Madras and Bengal – each had its own Governor and its own Army. The Presidency Armies were under the control of the Governor. In 1748, the C-in-C of Bengal Army was also appointed C-in-C of India.

In 1773 the British Parliament passed the Regulating Act under which a Governor-General was appointed for India and he became the supreme authority of the British in India. The Governor-General was given a Council of four members. The C-in-C was one of the four members of the Governor-General's Council. In 1786 a Military Department was constituted under a Military Member. He was also included in the Governor-General's Council. The Military Department became the focal point which used to communicate the orders of the Governor-General in Council to the three Presidency armies. All proposals coming from the three Armies for consideration by the Governor-General in Council had to be sent through him. The Military Department became the link between the Governor-General and the three Presidency Armies. The control of the C-in-C was confined primarily to operational matters.

The Military member commented on all proposals sent by the C-in-C to the Governor-General, before the government took a decision and communicated the government decisions to the Army. When Kitchener was appointed the C-in-C he found the style of functioning in government most unsatisfactory. He pressed for the removal of the Military Member, who was of Major-General rank. Curzon was opposed to this suggestion but ultimately Kitchener had his way. The Military Member was dropped from the Council and the Department was re-designated as the Army Department and came under the C-in-C directly This made the C-in-C all powerful. Lord Curzon called this as the creation of Military despotism.

However in 1906, the British Government created a Military Finance Department with the objective of maintaining financial control over military expenditure and making the department 'more constant and efficacious'. The C-in-C had to take the Military Finance Department's advice on the financial aspect of any military question, before "making a formal reference to the Department through the Military Finance Branch." The Secretary of Military Finance Department would be responsible only to the Honourable Finance Member and to his Excellency the Governor-General. This also provided a check on the authority of the C-in-C who had become all powerful.

The C-in-C was also an ex officio member of the Central Legislative Council and the Army Secretary an ex officio member of the Central Legislative Assembly.

The Esher Committee was set up by the British Government after the First World War to examine the position of the C-in-C in his dual capacity as head of the Army and Member of the Executive Council and to make recommendations. One of the recommendations was that the appointment of the Army Secretary be made tenable only by a civil servant. This was accepted and from 1921, officers from the Indian Civil Service started being posted to this office, which was later re-designated as Defence Secretary.

In October 1946 the Interim Government came into power and for the first time control over Defence was handed over to an Indian. Sardar Baldev Singh became the Defence Minister of the Executive Council with the Defence Secretary and the Defence Department under him. The C-in-C Field Marshal Auchinleck now ceased to be a member of the Executive Council and worked under the newly appointed Defence Minister. However he continued to be the professional Head of the three Services. After Independence, Lord Ismay, who was the Chief of Staff to Lord Mountbatten was tasked to examine the Indian higher defence organization. Ismay recommended a series of Committees for higher defence control, which would ensure the supremacy of the civil, provide maximum coordination between the Services and reduce red tape cutting out avoidable delays.

At the highest level there was the Defence Committee of the Cabinet (DCC) under the Chairmanship of the Prime Minister. The Defence Minister and certain selected ministers were members of this Committee. The three Service Chiefs, the Defence Secretary and the Financial Advisor were required to be in attendance at all meetings of the DCC.

Then there was the Defence Minister's Committee which was the apex body in the Ministry of Defence. Its members were the three Service Chiefs. The Defence Secretary and the Financial Advisor.

In 1952, the status of Armed Forces Headquarters were designated as 'Attached Offices' by the Cabinet Secretariat.

In 1955 the Service Chiefs who had continued to carry the designation of C-in-C were re-designated as Chief of Staff of their respective Service. Announcing this in Parliament on 25th March 1955, Jawaharlal Nehru stated –

> "It would be better if in future the designation of the Commander-in-Chief should be dropped and they should be called the Chiefs of Staff.... It is proposed that the Heads of the Services in future be called Chief of the Army Staff, Chief of the Naval Staff and the Chief of the Air Staff...."

In 1962 the Cabinet Secretary was given higher protocol status than the Service Chiefs

All these developments have led to a feeling in the defence officers that their status has been downgraded. They feel it is the civil bureaucracy which is behind all this. They also feel that the successive Pay Commissions, starting from the Third Pay Commission, which reduced the pensions of defence officers to the same as the civilian officers, that is 50%, has reduced their status.

This feeling is not there at the highest levels but is widely prevalent in the middle levels and junior levels. After the Seventh Pay Commission this feeling has further increased on account of allowances as well as the pay scales.

Decision-Making in the Defence Ministry

Decision-making in the Defence Ministry is conditioned by the following factors:

1. It is like any other Ministry/Department of the Government of India with the Secretary, Defence, being the Chief Accounting Officer responsible for the expenditure of funds to the Parliament.
2. It is a Ministry which controls all the fighting arms of the Defence forces, and therefore urgency is involved in decision-making in all respects.

3. The Headquarters of the three forces i e of the Army, Air Force and Navy take certain decisions at their own level under their delegated powers and only refer those cases to the Ministry of Defence which are not included in the delegation.
4. In this decision-making, apart from the main department of Defence, which looks after the three armed forces, there are three other Secretaries and Departments who are to be consulted off and on in decision-making, namely the Department of Defence Production and Supplies, the Department of Defence Research, i e the DRDO and third the Defence Finance.

The Defence Ministries all over the world are treated as holy cows. Their work is traditionally secretive in nature and involves a lot of confidentiality. Most of the files are 'specified' and their movements rigorously watched. Their movements are governed by the principle of 'need to know' and are not allowed to be circulated to all.

The outlays of the Defence Ministry in India are always the highest, and public and audit scrutiny of expenditure, specially relating to defence procurement are closely scrutinized. In such an atmosphere, decision-making in the Ministry is one of extreme responsibility and caution, both in the sphere of finances as well as administration, including the personnel management.

Defence forces, all over the world, are treated with deference and natural respect. After all they guard our borders, lay down their lives, fighting the enemies and are the last recourse in fighting the non-State actors, both within the country and outside.

Decision-making in the Defence Ministry, therefore has also to ensure that the morale of the officers is never down, they get adequate supplies of ammunition, weapons, uniforms in time; their budgetary requirements for maintenance of equipment, including supply of fuel and food are fully met. It can brook no delay.

At the same time the Defence Secretary, as the Chief Accounting Officer of the Ministry, responsible to Parliament for the moneys spent, has to ensure that the expenditure incurred is in accordance with the rules and budgetary provisions; and procedures are strictly followed while giving sanctions.

The interventions by the Ministry, on the recommendations made by the Chiefs/Defence Headquarters, are made only in those cases where the proposals are not conforming to the above.

During war, the Defence Ministry has to ensure internal coordination with Departments like Ministries of Railways, which looks after movements of the forces, the Department of Petroleum which looks after fuel supplies as well as Department of Finance, for provision of adequate funds. The Defence Ministry can sanction proposals/projects only within the financial powers delegated to it. Beyond the delegated powers it must go to the Finance Ministry and the Cabinet, wherever necessary. This often delays decision-making in the ministry but ensures financial probity in expenditure.

The civilian bureaucracy is derided for the delays in decision-making. The Defence Ministry is criticized by the defence officers for the proposals pending for a long time in the Ministry. The defence headquarters would like their proposals to be examined and approved at the shortest time possible. The Joint Secretaries in the Ministry however feel that proposals that come from the field take a long time in being processed in the service headquarters itself for which no criticism is made. However as soon as the proposal is sent to the Defence Ministry, the defence headquarters became critical of any delay. Moreover, after the Bofors purchase scandal and the exposure in 'Tehelka', the officers in the Ministry want to follow all procedures as laid down in the rules and manuals. The observations of the CAG in cases where deviations have been made, lead to a lot of work, as officers of the Defence Ministry have to defend the action taken by their predecessors before the Public Accounts Committee. Therefore the thinking is to play safe and follow the bureaucratic path.

Senior Appointments in the Defence Forces

Government keeps a control over the higher levels of appointments. All appointments on posts equivalent to Brigadiers and above are vetted by the Defence Ministry for consideration of the Appointments Committee of the Cabinet. Normally the practice in the Ministry is to go along with the recommendations of the Boards, existing in the Armed Forces Headquarters, usually headed by the concerned Chief. However if the Defence Ministry gets an adverse input, or already has something on a person's dossier, it can ask for reconsideration. In the Defence Ministry we want to avoid conflicts on such recommendations but our duty is also to keep the minister aware of all the facts. The Defence Ministry is often accused of interfering in the proposals sent by the Armed Forces Headquarters but there is no way the Ministry can avoid looking into complaints received. Often when there are differences of opinion, recourse is taken to across the table discussions either at the level of the Joint Secretary or sometimes at the level of the Defence Secretary.

There was a peculiar case, in my time, when the new Air Chief was to be selected. The senior most officer of the Air

Force had, a fortnight back before the selection, while personally flying a fighter plane, crossed over the border and his plane was subject to a missile attack, which had damaged the plane. When he returned, with the damaged plane, he did not report the incident to his Air Chief. Later when an enquiry was ordered, he blamed the navigator. After taking further evidence, the Air Chief found him guilty and recommended action against him. This became a part of his personal file and he was thus passed over for the position of Air Chief. To the outside world it appeared as if the Defence Ministry had broken the principle of seniority but those who knew, agreed with the decision of the Ministry.

There has often been a demand that officers of the three defence forces should be included in the Ministry and become a part of the decision-making process. The concept of the three defence headquarters merely being called Integrated Headquarters of the Ministry of Defence does not satisfy the proponents of this concept. These demands have arisen from time to time but have not been accepted by the government. In my time a request was also made that one of the staff officers of the Defence Minister should be an officer from one of the forces. However, this was also not politically acceptable and the minister turned it down.

I have often wondered on the pros and cons of this proposal of posting officers of the armed forces in the Defence Ministry. The obvious advantage, prima facie, is the domain knowledge they would bring of their branch. A Naval officer would bring his knowledge of naval ammunition, running of ships, training of personnel, requirement of naval personnel etc. But he would not be having any domain knowledge of the Army and Air Force. So he will have to work only in the branch of the Ministry dealing with Navy. Furthermore if a proposal comes from the Naval Headquarters, would he be able to take an independent view? He knows that after a fixed tenure in the Ministry he will have to go back to the Navy and will be certainly looking over the shoulder. Furthermore armed forces officers cannot work in a regimental bureaucratic atmosphere where procedures are strictly followed on the files. He would also take time to learn how to deal with the Finance Ministry or the Law Ministry as well as follow the financial Handbook. Perhaps after some years he might be able to do all this but would feel more at home in the field where he can command, control, show his initiative and leadership and get his promotions. Carrying his files and trying to understand the nuances of the long notes written by the Under Secretary, Deputy Secretary, etc, would not be his forte. Perhaps a better and more appropriate posting for such Officers would be the headquarters of the force to which he belongs, as he can give out his best in a congenial atmosphere. Of course in Departments like Defence Research, where local knowledge of the requirement of the forces would help initiate research in the desired field, defence officers should be certainly posted, as they are even now.

Another problem which armed force officers often face, when they work with civilians, is the problem of equivalence and seniority. Whereas in the forces, ranks are very clear and protocol related to the ranks is very well laid down it is not so in the civilian side. The problem is also encountered in the headquarters of the armed forces, where civilians belonging to the AFHQ often fight for changing the equivalence laid down by the Ministry from time to time. The armed forces feel unhappy when their proposals are vetoed by the Section Officer of the Ministry or the civilian Under Secretary/Deputy Secretary at the Armed Force Headquarters. Whenever equivalence is laid down, the civilian officers also expect the officers of the forces lower down in the rank to salute them. This rarely happens.

I found that even the PROs of the Armed Forces, who normally come from the Indian Information Service, are not very comfortable in the environment they work in. Though they are given ranks and uniforms for easier accessibility and appropriate respect, they are dealt with rather shoddily by the regular officers of the armed forces. However even with the support of the PROs, the armed force officers do not feel very comfortable with the journalists, whose appetite for news is gargantuan in volume. Neither does an armed force officer want to be disturbed too often for giving information which is largely sensitive in nature.

The Armed Forces are trained to live away from civilians. They live in exclusive cantonments and work in their own military environment. They learn to give crisp orders, receive orders and implement orders. The only civilians they come in contact with in the district, are the civilian authorities, e g the District Magistrate, the Superintendent of Police the SHO or the civil contractors who supply food, vegetables or are registered for the engineering works with the garrison engineer. In the cantonments, the Cantonment Boards consist partially of civilians who are elected as per the Cantonments Act, and the defence officers nominated by the Services. The net result is, that these military officers feel uncomfortable in dealing with civilians. They need a modem, or an intermediary, to deal with civilians.

Military Officers have their own housing. In Delhi, as well as in some major metros, military officers have been allotted houses within the defence pool. Within the allotted pool, the military authorities themselves issue the allotment orders. Government earmarks large funds for constructing accommodation for the armed forces all over the country. In 2001 the Defence Ministry was mandated to go for large-scale construction of houses under the married accommodation category. The work was massive. A couple of months went into planning. Finally the programme was launched. Providing more and more official accommodation to the officers and men has been a consistent demand of the armed forces.

I must record my appreciation of Jaswant Singh, our then Defence Minister, who really took the initiative in starting this scheme. With his deep knowledge of defence forces (being himself a former army officer) he knew what was required urgently by the defence forces. Sri Jaswant Singh's knowledge of security and defence issues is deep and professional. His books reflect his incisive thinking and I would recommend them to anybody who wants to delve deep into such issues. I have read his books and found them extremely informative. He has written several books. Some have landed him into controversies but Sri Jaswant Singh believes in giving full expression to what he thinks right.

When Sri Jaswant Singh was the Defence Minister he would review the implementation of all the decisions he had taken, every week. All the Chiefs and all the Secretaries of the Defence Ministry were to be present. These meetings were very businesslike, I used to record the decisions and apprise the minister pointwise on the implementation of these decisions.

In one of the meetings, he announced that he would like to abolish the Department of Defence Estates. He gave no rationale for the decision except that several complaints had been received. Subsequently after the meeting I discussed this with the DGDE Veena Maitra. She was very stunned. I asked her to meet the minister. She did so but she came back to me and said that minister was adamant.

In the next weekly meeting of the officers, the Defence Minister wanted to know the action taken on the proposal. I told him that we are examining the proposal as we would have to consider who would look after all these properties belonging to the defence as well as to how the personnel would have to be readjusted. Then Sri Jaswant Singh dropped another bombshell. He also wanted the Remount and Veterinary units to be also abolished. In his opinion they were doing no worthwhile work and could be dispensed with. The Remount and Veterinary Corps had to manage large farms in which they cultivate fodder for the horses still being maintained by the Army as well as to look after the mules used for carrying heavy equipment and goods in forward areas. The department had grown up in the British times but in the modern age, really had no useful role to play. Horses were used only on ceremonial occasions and never in actual warfare. The Army did not really require its own milk production or vegetables which were grown on these large farms scattered all over India. While I did agree in principle with the minister's decision but I left it to the Army Chief to take a view as this Remount and Veterinary Corps came directly under Army Headquarters. The Army Chief in the subsequent meetings raised several issues and also asked for further time to consider the proposal. Sri Jaswant Singh wanted a time-bound programme for the disbandment of both the DGDE as well as the Remount and Veterinary Corps. I told Sri Jaswant Singh that it would not be easy to abolish these organizations as they had grown over the years to fulfil the role given to them. He said that he would like his decision to be implemented and would like to be apprised of the next steps. As we were working on the 'next steps', George Fernandez was suddenly reinstated as Defence

Minister and Sri Jaswant Singh continued, as before, to look after the External Affairs Ministry only.

Both the proposals of Sri Jaswant Singh were dropped by George Fernandez and both the Departments continued to exist as they were.

In retrospect I always had a feeling that somebody was prompting Sri Jaswant Singh to go ahead with these proposals. The Defence Forces have never liked the Department of Defence Estates as they feel that it acts as a barrier to the way they would like to utilize or manage Defence lands. They accuse the DGDE of corruption and mismanagement. This may be true but it was also pointed out by DGDE how large tracts of defence lands have either been turned into golf courses or allowed to be leased out and sold for non-defence purposes. In my opinion, the Department of Defence Estates should continue, as it is necessary to bring in some discipline and prevent the large scale misuse of these lands. 'Santushti' is a case in point. Originally meant to give support to war widows, over the years it has been practically handed over to non-defence personnel for running the shops. War widows have receded to the background. Whenever efforts were made to cancel such allotments, as they violated the condition of lease, the Chief of Air Staff would step in to persuade the Defence Minister to take a lenient view. Audit objections are overruled and the gross misuse of defence property and violation of lease deed continues to this date. Every year the audit brings out these facts but no action is taken because of the protective attitude of the higher echelons in the Services.

I must mention one incident that occurred when Sri Jaswant Singh became the Defence Minister. He inspected all the offices including the room of the Defence Secretary. The room of the Defence Secretary has a beautiful view of Rajpath as well as Parliament. Sri Jaswant Singh called me the next day and stated that he would like to sit in my room and I should move to the room of the Defence Minister. I was shocked. I told Sri Jaswant Singh that it would take some time to shift as I was going to Moscow the next day. He agreed. After a fortnight he again enquired whether I had shifted. I told him that it will take at least another fortnight. I then brought this matter to the notice of Sri Arun Singh who had been appointed as Advisor to the Defence Minister. He was surprised and asked me not to worry. He obviously was successful, as Jaswant Singh did not raise the issue again.

Defence Budget

The budget of the Ministry of Defence increases substantially every year. But the capacity to utilize those funds is lacking. Every year substantial funds are surrendered. Earlier when the economy of the country was weak, allocation to the Ministry of Defence was restricted. There was always a complaint that modernization of the forces is not taking place at a rapid pace. It is out of the capital budget of the Ministry that the new weapons and weapon systems are bought. Because of the cumbersome financial rules the Ministry is not able to fully utilize the Capital budget placed at its disposal and this always gave a handle to criticize the Defence Ministry. The three services are also very critical of the slow processes involved in procurement.

It was not only the pace of capital expenditure that was slow. The procurement of spare parts for existing equipment was also slow. The officials of the Ministry were however extremely cautious about sticking to the due process. The CAG reports, the newspaper criticism, the threat of CBI inquiries, the probing Parliamentary questions all continued to slow down the sanctions.

The proposals of the three services were, till 2000, received directly in the Ministry. They were vetted by the Defence Account Wing, as well as by the Joint Secretaries of the Defence Ministry looking after the individual services. A rough figure of how much the budgetary allocation would be given to us by the Finance Ministry and we would then prune the demands of the various services to fit within the allocation. These allocations within the total budget would be made after intensive discussion with the three services Headquarters. It was never arbitrary as sometimes pointed out.

After the reports and recommendations of the Group of Ministers set up, after the Kargil War, were finalised, a Defence Procurement Board was immediately set up in May 2001. I had decided that the reforms should be immediately carried out and, on my request, Sri Ajai Vikram Singh was appointed as the first Additional Secretary in-charge of the Secretariat of the Defence Procurement Board. Sri Ajai Vikram Singh was chosen as he had already worked in the Defence Ministry before and was also my Principal Secretary, Industries in Uttar Pradesh when I was Chief Secretary, Uttar Pradesh. He had an impeccable record and his integrity was highly respected. Ajai set up the Defence Procurement Secretariat in record time and people were really surprised when we had the first meeting of the Procurement Board. Sri Arun Singh, who had become the Adviser to the Defence Ministry, personally congratulated me in initiating the reforms so expeditiously.

The setting up of the Defence Procurement Board immediately speeded up the procurement process. All procurements were decided across the table in consultation with the three Vice-Chiefs and their representatives. Secretary Defence Accounts as well as the other Secretaries of the Defence Ministry stated their views in the Board meeting itself and therefore a lot of file work got eliminated. The results were seen in the first year itself when capital expenditure rose by 35% and there was less surrender of funds.

Here I must point out that the political commitment to defence is so intense that funds are never a problem. We were not able to spend as much as the allocations made. We were always assured by the Finance Ministry in the CCS meetings that more funds would be given, whenever we required them. Suffice it say that the Defence Ministry never experienced shortage of funds in the period I was working there.

As I peruse the defence budgeting outlays today, I find that the allocations have increased more than three fold. It is for this reason that procurement of weapons is going on at a rapid pace and India has become the most dominant player in defence procurement in the world.

Visit to Siachen

Soon after joining the Ministry, I learnt that my minister George Fernandez used to make frequent visits to Siachen. Before joining the Ministry, I had also learnt that when Fernandez came to know about the delays in procurement of essential equipment for our men in Siachen, he had sent the concerned officials of the Ministry to Siachen to enable them to experience the rigours of working in those inhospitable terrains. I decided to go to Siachen and requested the minister for permission. The minister was extremely happy. Arrangements were made by the Army for my visit.

I went to the room of General Padmanabhan to seek his advice on the visit in general. He gave me one advise which I still remember. "When in Ladakh and Siachen" he said "walk like a yak." I saw a yak moving in Ladakh, which was my first stop en route to Siachen. The yak moves slowly and ponderously. It never hurries. I realized what General Padmanabhan meant.

From Ladakh, the Army authorities flew me to the Base Camp. Here I was given warmer clothing to wear and I was briefed on Siachen. My shoes were also replaced with snow shoes. I was introduced to the officers and men based here. They all looked cheerful and confident. I generally discussed their problems. The only complaint they had was shortage of satellite telephones which was the only method of contact with their families. They also pointed out the shortage of aircraft to take them to their home towns as the planes which flew them out were far and few. They also pointed out that often the waiting period was so long that often their leave would be just about finishing when they got their flights back. I noted all these difficulties faced by them.

I was then put in a Chetak helicopter. It is a single engine helicopter but is excellent in operations at these high altitudes. I was given heavy gloves to wear, as the outpost in Siachen would be extremely cold. After the helicopter took off, the only means of talking was the internal communication lines in the helicopter.

I looked down below on the snowy wastelands. In some areas I saw lot of rubbish on the snow as well as some dark brown substance. On enquiring I was told that it was human waste. The excreta remains in its original form as no bacteria survives to finish it. I saw miles and miles of this human waste. I was informed that the camps, where the soldiers lived, have to be shifted periodically to avoid the human remains.

There was literally no blade of glass on the glacier. It was just a solid mountain of ice. I was wondering how the helicopter would land. As the helicopter came down to a lower level, I noticed a square steel plate, placed on six drums below. I was told that the helicopter would land on top of this small platform and if the helicopter went even slightly left or right it would fall off the platform into the snow. Kudos to the pilot. He landed at the exact position. We were told not to take off our gloves because if we touched the steel door of the helicopter with bare hands, the flesh would just get stuck to the steel frame.

On getting down we were welcomed by cheerful faces of the officers and jawans. We were given warm juice to drink. They seemed quite excited and were eager to make me feel at home. I chatted with them. They showed me the places where they lived. Kerosene was the life line which gave them warmth as well as hot drinks and food. These houses of snow were small in size and, it seems, engendered the camaraderie which kept them alive. All for one and one for all.

The enthusiasm and cheerfulness of the men posted in these forbidding surroundings taught me a lesson. We can create happiness anywhere if we want to. It is the spirit and thinking that matters, not the external world. Caught between the open skies above and the mountains of snow below and the enemy in front, these men reflected the sturdiness of the human spirit.

I was offered a ride on the snow scooter. This is the only vehicle that operates in that frozen area. It helps in maintaining contacts with the out posts which are further away in the peaks. It was a lovely ride as we wove our way to a forward post and back. It was also a source of recreation for the men. I realized the importance of snow scooters and I firmly made up my mind to sanction more of them for our soldiers here.

I could hear the shelling from the other side. Our men would also respond and then change positions otherwise they might be blasted. I was told about the absence of weapon locating radars with the Indian Army. Pakistan already had them and could easily identify our positions. I noted this mentally.

After staying with them for some time and talking to them freely. I was told to get back on the helicopter as otherwise it would get dark. I sadly moved towards the helicopter engulfed in thoughts. Why do we send our men here in the wasteland of snow? Can we ever stop this fighting between the two nations, who were one at the time of partition, and were at each other's throat now? The constant shelling, the continuous fear of death. Yet these men were happy and cheerful. I saluted the Indian Army from my heart.

We came back to the Base Camp where we had snacks. Thereafter I was asked to address the men. I did so and thanked them for their dedication and service to the nation. Rounding off with a Jai Hind, I stepped on the helicopter once again and in the midst of waving of hands, started my journey back to Delhi.

Invitation to My Wife for Launching a Ship of the Indian Navy in St Petersburg

The Naval Chief one day sought an appointment with me and walked into my office at the appointed time. He informed me that a new ship ordered by the Indian Navy was ready to be handed over to India in the dockyard at Saint Petersburg, Russia. As usual there will be a ceremony in which a lady has to formally launch the ship. He was wanting to know whether my wife would be willing to do so. If I agreed then he would send a formal proposal to the Defence Ministry for the same.

I was extremely overwhelmed at this kind gesture. I checked up with my wife and she was of course, quite delighted with the proposal. I conveyed her consent to Admiral Sushil Kumar, the then Naval Chief.

The proposal duly came to the Defence Ministry. The office pointed out that it was the first time that such a proposal had come, as the wife of a Defence Secretary had never been called to launch a ship before. It involved government bearing the cost of my wife's ticket, as she would be going on government expense to St Petersburg and staying there. The office said, in any case the proposal would have to go through the Defence Minister, and after obtaining his concurrence, would be sent through the Finance Ministry and to the Prime Minister for approval. Jaswant Singh, our Defence Minister, with a very open outlook and an open-hearted approach, fully endorsed the proposal. The proposal went to the Finance Ministry for onward transmission to the office of the Prime Minister. In the meantime I had to proceed to Moscow for the annual Indo-Russia Defence talks. While I was in Moscow, Ajay Prasad my Additional Secretary Defence rang me up saying that the proposal for my wife's visit had been rejected by the Prime Minister and the file had come back. I told him to show the file to the Defence Minister and seek his guidance on the matter. Ajay Prasad rang me back the next day saying that the Defence Minister had felt personally very bad as he felt a proposal, endorsed by him, had been rejected by the PMO without any valid reason. The Defence Minister therefore put up another note under his own signature, asking for reconsideration of the proposal by PMO. The file never came back, but Jaswant Singh informed me that the Prime Minister telephoned him on this matter and asked him not to press the matter as it would set a precedent for other Ministries. I thanked Jaswant Singh for all his efforts and dropped the proposal from my mind. I however carried this impression that probably it was Ajit Singh the Finance Secretary who had rejected the proposal. Ajit Singh had been a former Defence Secretary, not very popular with the Defence forces. A number of controversies had cropped up in his time and the relations were reported to be at an all the time low between the Defence Ministry and forces during his tenure.

Kargil War

The Kargil War took place in May-July 1999. There was no build up to this war. It was only when some shepherds on the Indian side, informed the Army, of the intrusions of some Pakistani soldiers in Kargil, that the Indian Army got alerted. The first probing Indian Patrol never returned. The Army Chief was abroad. However the Indian media picked it up and the Army suddenly discovered that the Pakistani soldiers were now well-settled on the Indian side. As the attempts to dislodge the Pakistani soldiers increased, the Indian Army found severe shortages in various equipment, ammunition, clothes, night vision goggles, winter clothing shoes etc. Our soldiers were hard put to scaling the hillsides while the Pakistani outposts were securely established on the top and kept on firing on them.

When the Kargil War was on, I was Chief Secretary in Uttar Pradesh. To boost up the morale of the troops passing through Uttar Pradesh, either by trains, or by road, huge welcome arches were put up, and sweets given to the jawans. The bodies of several officers and jawans who were casualties in the war came in draped coffins. The District Magistrates were directed to be personally present and have the bodies cremated with full honours. Like every other State, we also announced compensation for the families of the jawans. We compared the compensation being given by other states, and endeavoured to be better than them. Donations freely flowed in for the Kargil War Fund. The war was being keenly watched inside every home, which had a television set. We heard the analysis by experts, watched our jawans firing at the forward Pakistan posts and felt proud, when our officers and jawans reconquered the peaks one by one. The whole nation was one.

After the Kargil War, the government set up a Committee under the well-known defence expert K Subramanian to analyse and give its recommendations on the measures that should be taken to meet such situations. On the basis of this report, the government set up a Group of Ministers under LK Advani to give its considered view as how to make the armed forces more effective. In turn this Group of Ministers set up four task forces, one under Godbole (former Home Secretary), second under NN Vohra (former Defence Secretary), third under Sri Arun Singh (former Minister of State for Defence) and the fourth under GC Saxena to analyse the problems concerning Border Management, Internal Security, Management of Defence and the Intelligence agencies respectively and to give their recommendations on the entire gamut of National security while taking into account the need for flexibility in the context of newly emerging challenges.

The reports of the task forces were then presented to the Group of Ministers consisting of LK Advani, George Fernandez, Jaswant Singh and Yashwant Sinha. I became Defence Secretary in October 20, 2000 and participated in the deliberations of the Group of Ministers together with the Home Secretary and the heads of the four Task Forces who were assisting the Group of Ministers in finalizing their recommendations. It gave me an excellent opportunity to get acquainted with the complex issues concerning national security. I also gave my own practical inputs from the field, especially on Civil military relationship.

The report of the Group of Ministers was then presented to the Cabinet Committee on Security headed by the Prime Minister.

Here it is relevant to mention that during this period, in one of the meetings of the Consultative Committee on Defence, I was asked questions about the recommendations of the Group of Ministers. I stated that as the reports had just been presented to the Prime Minister and was to be discussed by the CCS I could not make public the recommendations as yet. Then the members asked me about the recommendations pertaining to the appointment of a Chief of Defence Staff (CDS) and the views of the Government of India on setting up of a Chief of Defence Staff for the defence forces. I said that a view could be taken on this issue only after the CCS had deliberated on it. It was then that the late Sri Madhavrao Scindia and Sri Romesh Bhandari, along with some other members of the Congress party got up and stated that they were strongly opposed, to the setting up of the Chief of Defence Staff and their views should be placed before the CCS, whenever it convenes to deliberate on this issue. I promised to do so.

After some days the CCS was convened to deliberate on the recommendations of the Group of Ministers. As soon as the question of Chief of Defence Staff cropped up, I told the members of the CCS of the views of the Consultative Committee and what I had been asked to convey. Prime Minister Atal Bihari Vajpayee also appeared to have received some communications from other sources in this regard. He stated that this matter be deferred as it would require further political deliberations. All the other recommendations of the GOM were approved except the one relating to the Chief of Defence Staff. The meeting thereafter concluded.

It was no secret in the defence establishment that while the Army was all for setting up of the Chief of Defence Staff, the Navy was undecided, while the Air Force was opposed to it. No wonder therefore that the recommendations of the Government of India to set up Chief of Defence Staff was deferred while all other recommendations were agreed to. This initiated a strong debate in the defence forces as well as the media, some for and some against. Anyway a historical opportunity to set up a Chief of Defence Staff, on the pattern of Australia, UK and USA, was lost.

One of the major recommendations of the Group of Ministers was on setting up of a Defence Procurement Board to speed up purchases of military hardware and equipment. Central to this was the appointment of a Special Secretary (Procurement). I was very keen to get this part of the Report implemented immediately as I was conscious of the accusation against the Defence Ministry for the delays in procurement. We were lucky to identify an officer Sri Ajai Vikram Singh, who had earlier served in the Defence Ministry, for this job. Within a week of the acceptance of the recommendations of the CCS I got Ajai Vikram Singh appointed as Special Secretary (Procurement). Sri Arun Singh, our Adviser in the Defence Ministry was very surprised at this promptness and as stated above complimented me for the same through a letter which I have jealously preserved. We also set up an Implementation Cell, to implement all the recommendations of the Group of Ministers. This facilitated matters and speeded up the implementation of reforms in various areas. Admiral Madanjit Singh of the Navy and Major-General

Chopra of the Army played a vital role in the implementation of the recommendations. Even the delegation of powers – both financial and administrative were issued after intensive deliberations with the three defence headquarters in the same year. The Integrated Defence Staff Headquarters was also promptly set up. The Army Headquarters, the Navy Headquarters and the Air Force Headquarters were also re-designated as Integrated Headquarters of the Ministry of Defence in accordance with the recommendations. By this step, the Service Headquarters were brought, psychologically closer, to integration with the Ministry of Defence.

The implementation of the reforms approved by the CCS had another positive fallout. Earlier a grievance of the Defence officers, at the highest level, used to be that they had no access to the Defence Minister and therefore were unable to put up their view points. Now with the setting up of the Defence Acquisition Council, headed by the Defence Minister, in which the three Chiefs were members, they had direct access to the minister. Apart from this the Vice-Chiefs were members of the Defence Procurement Board and thus directly participated in procurement. The Price Negotiating Committee also had a Major-General or equivalent rank officer to negotiate and participate in the tendering process. We also have a weekly meeting with the minister in which all the three Chiefs as well as all the Secretaries in the Ministry of Defence participate, together with the Secretary, Ministry of External Affairs and occasionally the Cabinet Secretary. Thus accessibility to the minister is much more than before, for the Defence Chiefs and other senior officers of the Defence forces.

The setting up of the Defence Procurement Board was a positive step. The Vice-Chiefs regularly attended these meetings with their advisers and other staff. Defence Secretary presided. Decisions were promptly taken. In one year alone we managed to increase capital expenditure on procurement of new equipment, as stated earlier, by more than 35%.

A Tri-Service Command was also set up for the strategic management of nuclear assets. Detailed orders were issued finalizing the chain of command. Similarly a Tri-Service Command was set up to manage the forces of the Army, Air Force and Navy looking after the security of the Andaman and Nicobar islands.

We found that while each of the defence forces functioned effectively while working alone, but when they were asked to coordinate and work as one, they would be finding faults with each other. This pin pricking did not occur at the higher levels but only at the middle and lower levels. Rank consciousness and force consciousness is indeed very high at the middle and lower levels. It was brought to my notice, at that time, that both in USA and Australia, it took almost thirty years to integrate the three wings of the Armed Forces into one whole. Ultimately it had to be done by legislation in both the countries. In India we are presently enforcing this closeness and coordination on the basis of governmental orders issued from time to time. Perhaps this will not do. Eventually a legislation would be necessary to legally enforce closeness and coordination within the armed forces. More than fifteen years have passed since defence reforms were introduced but, except in defence procurement, the closeness and coordination has not been achieved in the remaining sectors.

The reason is also historical. The envy is also historical. When the East India Company came, they brought with them people from Britain but no Armed Forces. Eventually as they began to expand beyond trading, to acquisition of territories and battles like the Battle of Plassey occurred, the need of having trained soldiers to back up the acquisition of territory arose. Each of these Presidencies ie Calcutta, Bombay and Madras had developed their own armies and trained them to use sophisticated arms. Each of these Presidency armies had their own Army Chiefs. Later when instead of separate Governors for the three Presidencies, we had a Governor-General looking after all the three Presidencies, a Commander-in-Chief of the Army was appointed as overall commander of the Armed Forces under the East India Company. The Commander in Chief was also a member of the Viceroy's Council, in fact he was number two in hierarchy. At that time there was no separate Naval Chief or Air Force Chief.

In 1947 came Independence. Prime Minister Nehru first of all removed the Commander-in-Chief from the Cabinet as he said that in a civilian Cabinet the C-in-C had no place. Later the government also created a separate Chief for the Navy and a separate Chief for the Air Force. In this way they brought the three wings of the Defence Forces at par. But the rivalry between the forces continued, as the Army wanted to assert its superiority and the other two forces were not willing to accept the Army as anything but equal.

When I came to the Defence Ministry I also learnt that after the 1971 victory in Bangladesh, the Army wanted to claim it as their victory, but the Air Force felt it had played an equally important role. They resented the claim of the Army. When the recommendation for the creation of CDS was made, it was visualized that the CDS would not necessarily be from the Army but may be appointed from any of the three branches of the Defence Forces. However, the impression that was generated, was, that the CDS would be always from the Army and this did not go well with the Navy and the Air Force. This impression arose from the fact, probably, that whereas in the

Tri-Service Command to be set up in the Andaman, Nicobar islands as well as Strategic Command it was mandated that the board would be selected by rotation from all the three forces, it was not so specifically laid down for the CDS.

The organization under the Chief of Integrated Defence Staff also never became effective. It was originally proposed to set up this organization to serve under the CDS but when the post of CDS was not created, it was put under the Chairman of the Chiefs of Staff. But this necessarily weakened its strength, effectiveness and independence. Whereas the CDS was to be a five star general and act independently and without bias, the same could not be said for the Chairman of the Chief of Staff, as the Chairman would be always seen as biased towards the force, he belonged to. The Naresh Chandra Committee has recommended that the post of Chief of Staff Committee should have a fixed tenure, but this yet to be accepted.

The posting in the Integrated Defence Staff was also seen as a posting for mediocres and therefore IDS lost the effectiveness which automatically comes from the posting of senior and respected officers. The entire concept of the Integrated Defence Staff being manned by experts, and senior people who could effectively coordinate between the three forces and also ensure that the procurement of weapons and military platforms by each of the Armed Forces is balanced, and bring them at par as far as technology is concerned, could never materialise. The Integrated Defence Staff was also visualized as the final authority for recommending the Budget for the Armed Forces, to the Ministry, but in actuality this was never accepted by the individual forces. The concept of integration in the Armed Forces has still a long way to go before it becomes a reality. The concept of 'jointness' amongst the defence forces can never be forced, it has to gradually evolve.

In the USA and UK the concept of 'jointness' also got strengthened because their forces fought in for off places where coordination between the three wings was absolutely necessary. In India, our forces always operate within the borders (except once in Sri Lanka and Maldives). The Government of India has never allowed the forces to cross the national boundaries/Line of Actual Control. More often, jointness is necessary when there is an 'offensive' strategy rather than in defence mode.

During the Kargil War, when the Army started action on the high peaks of Kargil, the Air Force was not initially taken into confidence. It was only later that the Air Force was asked to support the Army and directed to do 'precision bombing', as the Government of India did not allow it to cross the border. The Air Force fully supported the Army. Action followed, with the results, which we are now proud of.

The Army has its own Air wing to give air support to any action on the field. The Army has been always wanting to expand and strengthen its air support wing. This has been strongly opposed by the Air Force, which feels that the operations in the Air should be left to them. Such pin pricks continue to affect the relationship between the two forces. The Navy has kept out of this 'inner conflict' though it also continues to have a strong Air wing consisting of helicopters, Dornier and other fixed wing planes, long distance reconnaissance planes etc. The Air Force usually does not approve of acquisition of air assets by the Navy.

The Army is numerically a stronger force with over 11 lakh personnel. Next comes the Navy and thereafter the Air Force. Tangible efforts have been made, both through the Integrated Defence Staff and other inter service organizations to achieve greater synergy and jointness amongst the three services and integrate policy, doctrine, technology and procurement. Tri Service joint exercises were conceptualized in 2002 but the first such joint exercise was carried out, under the aegis of the IDS, only in October 2009, about seven years after the reforms were initiated in the defence sector.

The Tehelka Expose

One evening my Additional Secretary, Ajay Prasad, hurriedly rushed to my room asking me if I had seen the TV. I said 'No'. He informed me that a news channel had been airing the news since afternoon that people should watch a special telecast in the evening, involving the Defence Ministry. This programme had apparently been aired on the TV and telephone bells had started ringing. I opened the TV in my office and saw glimpses of the Tehelka expose, showing defence officers of the Army as well as some civilian officers of the Ministry accepting bribes. There were some shots of a room in a Hotel where an Army officer was being offered drinks. I immediately rang up the Vice-Chief of Army, Lieutenant-General Vij and asked him to initiate a probe.

I also asked Ajai to find out whether we could get a copy of the tapes from the TV Channel. Ajai returned after some time carrying a photostat copy of the dialogues which had been circulated to the news agencies. While I was going through the documents, and noting down the names of the officers involved, the telephone from the Defence Minister came. He was wanting some action to be taken during the night before Parliament convened next day. The video tapes were of four and a half hours duration and edited from over 11 hours of filming.

It was already 6 PM in the evening. What could be done? I discussed with Ajai and it was decided that we would summon the officers whose names had appeared in the tapes immediately. But how do we summon these officers? We decided to take the help of the Director-General of Military Intelligence. I asked him to find out where these officers were, and call them over to my office for recording their statement.

One by one the officers came to my office. I would ask them if they had seen the Tehelka tapes on the TV. I would give them a blank sheet of paper and ask them to simply give their comments as for as it related to them. Those who had not seen the tapes on TV were given the transcript and asked to scrutinize the dialogues and the conversation and then give their comments. I used to tell all of them that I am not going to ask any question, neither would I query them on what they had written. Simply their comments.

All the officers were very cooperative. They came, wrote what they wanted to write and went away. This continued throughout the night. I telephoned my wife at 10 PM informing her of the developments and telling her that I would come very late. I never expected that it would go on till morning.

The Army Chief was not present but I was keeping the Vice-Chief General Vij informed about the developments. I went through each statement. While all others denied their involvement, one officer, Major-General Chowdhury was the only one who accepted the fact that he had taken one lakh of rupees for advising the Tehelka people on how to compete for procurement. When I saw his statement, as he handed it over to me. I asked him whether he was making it of his own free will. He said that he was, because as an Army officer he felt he must be honest. He also mentioned that a retired senior colleague of his had called him to meet the Tehelka people, so he could not refuse. His retired senior colleague had also asked him to accept the money which he did. I had no comments to make. But his candid confession left me confused because in some respects, I did admire General Chowdhury for his honest admission.

It was 6 o'clock in the morning. I had not gone home and neither had Ajai or the DGMI. We had called for simple 'Roti' and 'Dal' from outside (as the office canteen had closed) for dinner. My wife had kept on ringing me up from time to time and I had told her that I could not come, till the entire exercise is finished.

In the morning the Defence Minister rang up as he was wanting to make a statement in Parliament. I had already anticipated this and I told him we are preparing it and will give it to him when he comes to office. I also informed General Vij about the statement and the confession by General Chowdhury. I asked him to take appropriate action under the rules in view of the candid admission of accepting one lakh rupees. General Chowdhury was relieved of his duties immediately.

The statement for Parliament was finalized and handed over to the Defence Minister. Thereafter I left for home to have a bath and freshen myself.

As Parliament convened, the opposition parties raised the issue of Tehelka tapes and wanted to know the action taken. The Defence Minister read out the statement and also informed Parliament about the action taken against General Chowdhury. In the meantime the civilian officers of the Ministry of Defence, including the Additional Secretary whose name had figured in the tapes, were also asked to give their explanation. The Additional Secretary confirmed that the Tehelka group had sought an appointment, but after meeting them he had told them that he had nothing to do with defence procurement. He denied having accepted any article/ necklace from them though they did offer him, as shown in the tapes.

The Army meanwhile took prompt action against all the army officers shown in the tapes. They were either relieved of their charges, or suspended. The prompt action did lessen the criticism in the press but the adverse impact created on defence purchases remained. Government announced the formation of a Committee under a retired judge of the Supreme Court Justice K Venkataswami, to investigate the entire affair and identify the guilty.

The notification for the Committee was urgently issued and Justice K Venkataswami came to Delhi to start the enquiry. He was temporarily put up in the guest accommodation at the India International Centre. I went to receive him and assured him of full cooperation in the enquiry. Ajay Prasad was made the nodal officer in the Defence Ministry to ensure supply of all files and documents required by the one man Commission. Sri Gopal Subramanian, a well-known Senior Lawyer was appointed to assist the Commission. All the original files required by the Commission were sent to them.

The Commission started taking evidence of the officers mentioned in the tapes. I was told by Ajay, that all those summoned were intensively questioned by the Commission and by Sri Gopal Subramanian. There were allegations and complaints made on the functioning of the Commission and its Chairman. Files stacked up in the Chairman's office. They were bulky files and we were all wondering how the Commission would sift through the files. The Commission continued to function for months together. Judges are used to a very slow style of functioning. Ajay used to brief me and the Defence Minister of the developments. He used to also occasionally attend the sittings of the Commission. After some time it became more or less a routine affair for the Ministry.

In June 2002, when I left the Ministry, the Commission was still carrying on its enquiry. Later the Judge was changed by the government in 2003 and another Judge, Justice SN Phukan was appointed. Subsequently, when the UPA government came to power, the Commission of Enquiry was closed as it was leading to nowhere. The incomplete Phukan Committee report was tabled in May 2005. It found no irregularity or illegality in any of the past transactions of finance deals that had been identified for investigation by the Venkataswami Commission. The investigation into the Tehelka tapes was then handed over to the CBI. In 2006 CBI registered an FIR against Bangaru Laxman and others. After taking evidence, a Special CBI Court in 2006 found Bangaru Laxman guilty of taking a bribe in a fictitious defence deal and sentenced him to a four year term of imprisonment.

However the Army, court-martialed its officer, who was seen taking a necklace. I had to go and give evidence also. In the Ministry one officer was charge-sheeted and punished. Some went to court and got themselves exonerated.

The entire Tehelka tapes was a sting operation on how defence procurement can get perverted by greedy officers. However there was actually no equipment to be sold or bought. That was its weakness. It still remains a mystery why this sting operation was carried out. It would have been better received if the sting operation was carried out in an actual procurement case. The case also lost its sheen, when, the person behind the Tehelka tapes was himself caught in a sex escapade in Goa, some years later!

Visit to DRDO Laboratories in Bengaluru and Hyderabad

As part of my keenness to know about the different aspects of the working of the Ministry of Defence. I requested Dr Atre, Scientific Adviser to Raksha Mantri and Secretary, Department of Defence Research for arranging a visit to his research laboratories. He suggested that I visit Bengaluru and Hyderabad.

I was extremely impressed with the scientific research going on. Over the years, India had been able to build a very solid base for defence research. The defence scientists worked dedicatedly and with precision. The neatness and cleanliness in these laboratories, were exemplary. These laboratories are run in a very professional manner, and the management of these laboratories has evolved over the years. There is no interference by the government as such. The DRDO maintains close coordination with the three defence headquarters, at different levels, and then identifies the projects to be taken up. Some officers of the various areas of the defence forces are also taken on deputation and play a significant role in ensuring that the final research products meet the needs of these forces.

DRDO is often criticized for not providing the final products to the satisfaction of the defence forces. Fingers are pointed at the delay that take place. The DRDO, in turn, accuses the forces of rejecting their final products and preferring to buying equipment from outside. When I went to Avadhi (near Chennai) I was taken around the tank factory. The tank appeared ready and, as I was told, modified to meet the Army's requirements. But, according to the Director of the tank factory, at every final trial, some defect would be pointed out and the induction of these tanks (Arjun) would get delayed. We had recently agreed to the purchase of T-90 tanks from the Russians, and the Director DRDO felt that the Arjun tank would again be put in the back burner. Anyway it was a satisfying sight to see the standing tanks and the capacity of the country to produce its own equipment. Hats off to DRDO for giving the nation this feeling of pride.

In Hyderabad I was shown the Prithvi missiles and the Agni missiles which were ready for trials. I was also shown the anti-tank missiles which were still waiting acceptance by the Army. Dr Kalam had been responsible for the production of these missiles and I saluted him silently in my heart.

I was then taken to a secret and confidential place where scientists were working on an anti-missile missile. These missiles, like the Patriot missiles, used by the US in the Iraqi war, were planned to protect India from missile attacks from neighbouring countries. These were yet on the drawing board stage. Nobody at that time knew that India was quietly working on this missile. Eleven years later, in 2011, I read in the papers, that this missile, produced by the DRDO, has been successfully tested. It takes almost a decade to invent new defence systems, but different teams in the DRDO are working to meet the newly emerging defence requirements and make India self-reliant.

In Hyderabad an incident occurred, which I will always remember throughout my life. In one of the laboratories, which was developing the Nag anti-tank missile, the Director of the laboratory was personally showing me all the products produced. One of the missiles had come for repairs. While he was showing how the missile works, he put his fingers on a button on the missile (which later was found to be active) and the missile shot off. Right before our eyes the missile went through a wall. The whole room was full of smoke. People ran helter-skelter. This very room had several other anti-tank missiles stored and there was this fear that these missiles would also get activated. I was asked to run as far as possible away from the building. People were shouting. The fire brigade had been summoned.

I was put in a car and asked to move out. There was no knowing what might happen. I was taken to the residential quarters. There I was informed that two persons who had been standing in front of the missile had died. The danger was, that, if the remaining anti-tank missiles got activated, they would also shoot off in various directions. The complex we were in, also housed the Prithvi missiles. If, God forbid, they took off there would be a danger to the entire Hyderabad city and its people.

Within minutes, all the TV channels were showing details of the incident. I got frantic calls from Delhi asking about my welfare. I assured them of my safety. The IB was put on the alert to find out if it was a case of sabotage. The Police Commissioner of Hyderabad came frantically, to see me, and to get all the details. He said the IB in Delhi had directed him to come to me and see me and investigate the sabotage angle. The TV scenes were screening the place of incidence with all sorts of rumours and I thought that somebody must have informed my wife about the incident and she must be extremely worried. So, I rang her up and informed her that I was safe. By that time she had not seen the TV news and so was blissfully unaware.

Prompt action by the DRDO personnel and the Fire Brigade brought the situation under control quickly. The deaths of the two persons was unfortunate. But it brought home to me the danger under which our defence research scientists and their men are working.

Later while having lunch with the officers I asked the DRDO officials whether they had any trouble recruiting scientists for their jobs. They said that they had no problems in the initial recruitment, but they have problems in retention of these scientists as they are offered more lucrative jobs in the open market. However they pointed out that majority of the scientists also develop a sense of pride in working for their country and decide to continue.

Conferring the Designation of Marshal of the Air on Arjan Singh

A representation, signed by former Air Chiefs and other retired senior officers of the Air Force was received in the Ministry, demanding that former Air Marshal and former Commander in Chief of the Air Force Arjan Singh, should be conferred the designation of Marshal of the Air. This was on the lines of the designation given to Field Marshal Sam Manekshaw after the Bangladesh War. I had heard stories of the exploits of Arjan Singh during the 1965 Indo-Pak War. He was willing to bomb the Pakistan airfields all alone. He was, no doubt, a national hero, widely loved and respected.

I rang up Air Chief Tipnis and asked for his views. He fully endorsed the proposal. I then took the representation received, to the Defence Minister George Fernandez. He was himself an admirer of Arjan Singh and for the effective role played by the Air Force in the 1965 war under his leadership. He asked me to put up the formal proposal immediately.

I quickly wrote a note and marked it to the Defence Minister/Prime Minister and the President. I was surprised when the note was received back the next day, approved by all the three competent authorities. I then rang up Arjan Singh and apprised him of the decision of the government. Arjan Singh refused to believe what I had stated. He said that there must be some mistake. I told him there was no mistake. He enquired whether I was the Defence Secretary. I assured him I was and requested for an appointment to deliver the notification. He gave me time on the next day.

It was a privilege meeting him and his gracious wife. They were a lovely couple, so caring and affectionate. I will always remember them.

Arjan Singh always reminds me of the conversation we had on the telephone, when he thought that there was a mistake on my part!

Purchase of the Advance Jet Trainer

Several air crashes were taking place on the MiGs as well as the Mirages. Many air pilots had died in these crashes. While the analysis of the accidents showed that in some cases there was mechanical failure but in many cases it was attributed to human error. The pilots were not fully trained to fly these jet planes. There was no intermediate Jet trainer plane available with the Air Force. So the pilots moved from the simple trainers to fast moving Jets.

Around the mid-nineties the Air Force made a demand for Advanced Jet trainers. Request for proposals was floated. At the end of the day only two proposals were found fit. As negotiations were proceeding one of the proposals was withdrawn and only the British Hawk remained for price negotiations.

Air Marshal Inamdar was appointed as Chairman of the negotiating Committee. The negotiations dragged on for three years. The price recommended by DRDO was much lower than the offer given by the British Hawk company. Negotiations for lower prices was yielding limited results. Air Marshal Inamdar came to see me. I telephoned my counterpart, the British Secretary of Defence and requested him to persuade the British company to lower the prices. He said that he would discuss with the company and get back to me.

After some time the British Defence Secretary rang me up and said that the company has pointed out that it has already substantially reduced the prices and cannot go down further. I informed Air Marshal Inamdar about it.

Meanwhile the air crashes were continuing and young pilots were dying. There was uproar in Parliament whenever crashes were reported. I then requested the Defence Minister to call a meeting of all concerned. By this time the Air Chief Tipnis had retired. The new Air Chief came to the meeting. As I initiated the meeting and requested all concerned to take a decision on whether we should purchase the AJT at the lowest prices quoted by the company, Air Chief Krishnaswamy threw a spanner in the entire discussions. He stated that he does not approve of the engine of the AJT. So far, the Air Force had been strongly in favour of purchase of the British Hawk. The negotiations had been going on for the last four years and no issue of the engine had ever been raised. We were all stunned. The meeting ended abruptly without any decision being taken. Procurements in Defence get delayed for multifarious reasons, which we cannot reveal outside.

Kargil Purchases

In 2001, the CAG came out with a damning report on the purchases made during the Kargil War. The opposition clamoured for action against the Defence Minister, Sri George Fernandez, accusing him of corruption based on this report.

The Public Accounts Committee (PAC) immediately took up the matter. Date of hearing was fixed.

The Kargil War was fought in 1999 at the time of my predecessor TR Prasad, who later became the Cabinet Secretary. I went through all the files and the notings relating to the purchases. Except in one case, I felt that in all other cases pointed out by the CAG, the procurement procedures had been correctly followed and there was no evidence of corruption or wrong doings.

When I appeared before the PAC, I was fully armed with all the facts. The Congress MPs tried to corner me but I was successfully able to handle all the queries raised. I bluntly told the Public Accounts Committee that the purchases were fully justified and correctly made. The CAG, who assists the Chairman, PAC and sits by his side, was very surprised at my statement.

The hearings went on. Written replies were sent by the Ministry to the PAC on the questions raised. In the meantime, elections were to be held in Uttarakhand. The opposition took up a particular CAG para on coffins purchased from USA and called George Fernandez 'Coffin Chor'.

I had a deeper look at this particular file. I was shocked to see that the entire purchase was for ₹ 10 crore only and since it was within the financial powers delegated to the Defence Secretary, the files never went up to the Defence Minister. Furthermore, I found that the decision to purchase the coffins at the determined price was based on the recommendations of the Price Negotiating Committee (PNC) consisting of a Major-General rank officer of the Army, the Joint Secretary, Army and the Joint Secretary, Defence Accounts.

But politics has its own logic and strategy. The PAC could not come out with a unanimous report on the Kargil War purchases. The Chairman, PAC, Sri Buta Singh then took it upon himself to send the report.

When the opposition came to power, it decided to give the entire matter for investigation to the CBI. After three years of investigation, CBI could not find anything incriminating, except in one case. They submitted their report to the Supreme Court which accepted it without much ado.

However the harm had been caused. Officers were highly demoralized and decision-making became delayed. The officers were reluctant to participate in the purchase Committees. It was only after much persuasion that the pace of procurement again picked up.

But the entire incident left a bitter taste. Politicisation of defence procurement is a very dangerous strategy and benefits only the enemy. The opposition, (whichever political party is in it), must avoid damaging the morale of the officers of the Defence Ministry as well as the Armed Forces.

Kaluchak Massacre

On May 14th 2002 there was a terrorist attack near the town of Kaluchak in Jammu and Kashmir. Three militants reportedly crossed the Line of Control from Pakistan and boarded the bus at Vijaypur. When the bus neared Kaluchak, they shot the driver and the conductor and opened fire on the passengers. On hearing the shots in the bus, the Indian army soldiers fired in their direction. The terrorists, who were dressed in Indian army fatigues, returned fire and attempted to enter the Army's family quarters, located on the main road. They also threw grenades on some vehicles parked in the vicinity. Upon entering the family quarters, they again fired on Army members present in the premises. The terrorists were eventually cordoned and killed.

The death toll amounted to 36 killed, including three Army personnel, 18 Army family members and 15 civilians. The dead included ten children. All the three terrorists killed in this incident were Pakistani nationals.

It was almost the last straw and the Indian army was ready to attack Pakistan. However international pressure, though strongly against Pakistan, advised restraint.

The alternative of surgical strikes was planned. While leading a delegation to USA I met Rumsfeld, the Secretary Defence and asked him how USA would react if we carried out strikes against some Army and Air Force bases in Pakistan. Rumsfeld said that if India feels that such strikes are in national interest, he had no objection, but we must not attack any base where American troops were based, because if American troops were killed there would be a strong reaction. I informed Sri Fernandez accordingly.

Visit to Iran

As the Ministry of External Affairs was very keen to develop healthy relations with Iran. I went with a small team for defence talks with Iran. The atmosphere in Tehran was very conservative. I had read stories about Ayatollah Khomeini being the supreme voice of the country. There was not much crowd to be seen in the streets and the atmosphere was authoritarian.

While we were discussing the formal agenda laid down, their defence delegation head came to talk to me and sat next to my chair. He then made a request which shocked me. He said that Iran was very keen to acquire nuclear technology from India. I told him that we had a policy of non-proliferation and India had a consistent policy of not sharing our expertise in the production of nuclear weapons with any other country. At the end of an embarrassing discussion, he requested me to forward Iran's request to the powers that be.

I came back to the Indian Embassy and informed the Ambassador about the conversation. He informed me that Iran was trying to obtain nuclear cooperation from various countries. He also informed me that the Pakistan ambassador in Tehran was keenly following my visit and enquiring why I had come.

The Two Defence Ministers

George Fernandez and Jaswant Singh were exactly opposite to each other. While George Fernandez was extremely simple in every respect, Jaswant Singh had all the bearings and demeanour of an Army officer.

George Fernandez came to office, walking from his house. He shunned security. Inside the Defence Ministry he never used the lift and preferred to walk up the three floors. His room was bare and simple. Once he invited some officers of the Ministry to have lunch with him at his residence. It was simple dal, roti and some obscure vegetable. We saw his room, which only had a bed and a table. Under his pillow he used to place his clothes for them to be pressed. He used to wash his clothes himself.

Once the police security officer of the area came to see me and asked me to persuade George Fernandez to accept security as the police felt that he was a natural target for the terrorists. George Fernandez refused. When I went to persuade him he again refused. At the end I told the police that they should provide him security in a manner that is not visible. George Fernandez continued with his walk to the office.

Jaswant Singh, on the other hand was a man of fine sensibilities. He would have soft music playing in his room. There were several artifacts and paintings in his office. He talked with the graciousness of nobility. Soft spoken but hard-hitting. His dress was characteristic. Half rolled sleeves and a military sort of bush shirt, I have never seen him in a tucked shirt and pant. He would speak slowly and deliberately. Whenever he spoke in Parliament he had his right hand, half inside his bush shirt. They said that he had the photograph of his *'ishta devi'* in his inside pocket.

Both were very affectionate to all the officers of the Ministry. I guessed it was their backgrounds that were different. One was a rebel labour leader, who had almost brought the Railways to their knees. The other was a polished Army officer who had strayed into politics.

Farewell

My retirement was coming in June 2002. The Army Chief General Padmanabhan rang me up and said he would like to call on me. He came to my room and said that the Army had decided to give me a farewell. He said that when he enquired from his officers, they informed him that there was no earlier precedence. He asked me for a date and next morning sent a formal letter inviting me and my wife.

The farewell dinner was formal but lively speeches were made from both sides. General Padmanabhan mentioned in his speech that it was the first time that the Army was giving a farewell to a Defence Secretary. He expressed his admiration for the cooperation I had given. After the dinner, the officers carried me on their shoulders till my car. General Padmanabhan opened the door of the car and gave a Salute. I was thrilled.

It gave me immense satisfaction to learn that I had been accepted.

Chapter 9

Innings in Parliament

SOON after my retirement from the Ministry of Defence, I settled in my house in Noida. I had already had the re-tiling and renovation work completed. I had several request pending for lectures, symposia, participation in school functions etc. I now decided to chalk out my programme personally. I started off with Muzaffarnagar, whose people always gave me a lot of love and affection. I first of all attended the programme in the Bawaria Colony, where I had initiated development schemes to wean them away from a life of crime. Now a new generation of Bawariyas had come up. The problem however more or less, remained the same. Protests against police atrocities perpetuated by the local Thanedar, raids from across the border by the police of Haryana, who used to take away some of the younger Bawariyas forcibly, alleging that they were the ones who had committed burglary and dacoity in their area; confidential information about illegal distilling of liquor by the bad elements amongst the Bawariyas; request for protection and employment from those who had got educated and wanted to get away from their community. The local convener of the Bawariya development programme, Sri Kashyap who had worked with me, had kept me informed of all the development. We had worked hand in hand for the last twenty five years and brought several development schemes in the area. How could we let all these efforts made by us, wither away. We got the ADM (Additional District Magistrate) of Muzaffarnagar, who had accompanied us, to record all the requests/complaints made and to take prompt action on all of them.

Thereafter, I went to the main city of Muzaffarnagar. I paid obeisance to Swami Kalyandev, and got his blessings. Swamiji was a widely-respected social saint, whose sole mission in life was to improve society and to spread education throughout the region. Some of my acquaintances then took me, to a respected Jain Muni, who was spending his *'Chalisa'* in Muzaffarnagar. He was bare bodied and was sitting in a closed wooden enclosure, located in one of the rooms. I was introduced to him and I bowed respectfully. He blessed me three times with a fan. Thereafter I left.

On my way back to Delhi, as it was getting dark, I suddenly received a phone call on my mobile, from one of my most respected teachers, Gilbert Bose. He was my mathematics and geometry teacher in Boys High School Allahabad and we admired him for his clarity and helping nature. He had got my mobile number from a common friend. At first he congratulated me for my successful civil service career. He further said that since I had retired, I must enter politics, as the political environment needed clean, honest and dedicated people in India. I said I was hesitant to do so but he asked me to think about it at leisure. Then he conveyed his blessings once again and closed the talk.

A number of thoughts crossed my mind. The first was, what should I now do, after retirement? What are the things I had always wanted to do? I had read that on retirement, one gets the time to pursue, whatever one wanted to. What did I want? I was not sure. And then I remembered the blessings I had always received from my parents, elders and saints. I decided not to worry but let life play itself out.

While sitting in the balcony of my house, in the afternoon, my friend Anil Kumar telephoned me. He was also from Allahabad. He enquired as to what I was doing these days. I told that I am trying to find out how to live in my commuted pension of ₹ 7,800. I had to repay ₹ 6,000 per month also for the loan I had taken from the HDFC for buying this house in Noida. He asked me whether I would like to join as Secretary-General, Rajya Sabha. I was stunned and happily surprised. I said that I would love to do so. He asked me to come and see the Vice-President Sri Bhairon Singh Shekhawat, at Hyderabad House the next day.

I told my wife, who was equally happy. She did not like to see me idle in the house. The next day I got a telephone call from the Vice-President's office asking my car number and informing me about the time of the appointment. I went to Hyderabad House the next day, and met Sri Bhairon Singh Shekhawat. A tall man with a benign look, always smiling, he welcomed me. He asked me what I was doing and whether I would like to join as the Secretary-General of the Rajya Sabha. When I said 'Yes', he said that he was very happy and I should join tomorrow itself.

By the time I reached home, the telephone was ringing. It was my cousin Harshawardhan. He asked whether it was true that I had joined as Secretary-General, Rajya Sabha. I slowly said 'Yes' and enquired as to how he knew about it. He stated that it was already on the TV and the TV tickers were announcing the appointment. Thereafter, a number of telephone calls came congratulating me on my appointment. And thus my 'Innings in Parliament' started.

I went to see my room the next day, in Parliament. As I sat down, a number of Rajya Sabha officers and staff came to see me and pay their respects. The atmosphere was sedate but business like. The senior most officer Sri NC Joshi, gave me two books to read – one was *Rajya Sabha at Work*, the other was *Rules of Procedure in Rajya Sabha*. These two books proved invaluable to me throughout my tenure in Parliament.

The Secretary-General is the Chief Adviser to the Chairman, Rajya Sabha (Vice-President of India) on all parliamentary matters. Members of all political parties of the Rajya Sabha also approach him for advice on procedural matters. He is thus the advisor to the House. There is a large Secretariat under him and advice is given to the Chairman, based on rules and past precedents. The Secretary-General has to be completely impartial and apolitical while giving advice. He is the repository of the accumulated decisions and precedents of the House, the custodian of its conventions and traditions and a link between the changing membership of the House. He is a permanent officer of the House. But since the final action, based on his advice, is transparently and openly, acted upon in the House, the Secretary-General has to be fair and impartial. After taking his advice, the Chairman may finally decide to act in a particular manner, but for all his actions, the Chairman has to take the responsibility. No criticism of the Chairman or the Secretary-General, including the Rajya Sabha Secretariat, is allowed inside the House. If some member is unhappy, with a decision of the Chairman, or the Secretary-General, the matter can be raised in the Chamber of the Chairman but not in the House. The Secretary-General is responsible and answerable to the Chairman alone for his functions.

The functions of the Secretary-General are two-fold: parliamentary and administrative. Every day a meeting between the Secretary-General and the Chairman takes place before 11 AM. He has to be present when the members meet the Chairman with their spate of notices and mentions they want to make during the 'Zero Hour'. The notices which are admitted for the day are serially numbered as per the advice of the Chairman and are taken up serially during the Question Hour.

When the President arrives to address both Houses of Parliament assembled together, the Secretary-Generals of both the Houses, along with the Chairman, Rajya Sabha, Speaker Lok Sabha, Prime Minister and Minister for Parliamentary Affairs receive the President at the Gate of the Parliament House and come to the Central Hall in a procession along with the President. Similarly they join the procession when the President departs.

For the purpose of elections to the offices of the President and the Vice-President, the Secretary-Generals of the Rajya Sabha and the Lok Sabha are alternately appointed as Returning Officers. In my time, I was Returning Officer for the election to the office of Vice-President. I was privileged to receive the nomination of Sri Hamid Ansari in the Vice-Presidential Elections of 2007, given by no less a person than Dr Manmohan Singh. It was a thrilling experience to see the Hon'ble Prime Minister in my room.

The Secretary-General is the final authority on the admissibility of Questions raised by Members of Parliament. The balloting of questions is done in the presence of Members of Parliament but rarely does any MP come at the time of balloting. They have full faith in the Rajya Sabha Secretariat. But on the admissibility and rejection of questions, protests are often raised. Though the rules on admissibility are very clearly laid down, even then, on the interpretation of the rules, sometimes, the Members of Parliament raise questions. Normally the members are satisfied after they have met the Secretary-General, who calls for the file and explain why the Secretariat decided not to admit the questions.

I remember once, Vijay Mallya (erstwhile Chairman of Kingfisher Airlines) was unhappy because though he was balloted in Question Number 1, his question was disallowed because a similar question had been asked before. He raised the matter before the Chairman, who, after hearing him as well as the Secretariat, upheld the decision of the Secretary-General based on rules.

Sometimes questions are asked by members, based on the request of friends, who are keen to show their rivals in bad light. I remember Sri Ashok Chauhan of Amity University bringing this to the notice of the Chairman. Instructions were immediately issued to the Question Branch to be very careful and extra cautious in this respect. It is surprising how sometimes Members of Parliament are used by corporates as part of their inter-corporate warfare.

In fact the issue of paying money for raising of questions to help a particular party has been raised repeatedly in the media as well as the government. On 12th December 2005 the matter of acceptance of money by Members of Parliament in raising questions come to light in December after an expose in a television news channel showing MPs accepting money for tabling notices of Parliamentary questions. The Lok Sabha expelled ten of its members on the basis of the finding of an ad hoc Committee set up for this purpose. The Rajya Sabha first suspended the members and after a detailed examination of the conduct of the members by the Ethics Committee under Dr Karan Singh, expelled the concerned members.

Similarly on 19th December 2005 another private channel, telecast a programme titled 'Operation Chakravyuh' challenging improper conduct of some Members of Parliament in the implementation of the Members of Parliament Local Area Development (MPLAD) scheme. The matter was again referred to the Ethics Committee under Dr Karan Singh. The committee recommended in March 2006 that one of the two members whose name was mentioned be expelled. The House accepted the recommendation.

Acceptance of Gifts by Members When on Tour

The Chairman Rajya Sabha had been getting continuous complaints that Members of various Parliamentary Committees, while on official tours with the Committee, were getting expensive gifts from the PSUs and government department they were examining. In some cases the MPs were also demanding gifts. The Chairman was extremely concerned as it was adversely effecting the image of Parliament.

In consultation with some members and myself, guidelines were framed, for being followed by the Members which *inter alia* contained –

(a) The Departments/PSUs were directed to make arrangements for stay of the Committee members in State Guest Houses or Inspection Houses. Only if these were not available, would the arrangements be made in suitable Hotels.

(b) Lavish hospitality was to be avoided and only simple food should be served. No banquets allowed.

(c) At the time of departure, if the concerned department/ PSU does want to make a symbolic gift it should be of small value. Expensive gifts should not be given.

(d) If the member desires to have some goods purchased, he should pay for it.

Though these instructions were circulated to all members, it was difficult to enforce it as no department/PSU was willing to come forward and complain.

Questions in Parliament

Once a question listed at Number 1 in the list of starred question asked for the number of Hindus living in Pakistan. The State Minister for External Affairs telephoned me that his Ministry did not have the desired information and that this question should not be listed. He then sent a letter reiterating the same fact. I tried to contact the Chairman throughout the evening, but he was not available. To avoid any embarrassment and confusion in the Question Hour, the next day, I de-listed the question. The member, whose question it was, complained to the Chairman. I explained to the Chairman and showed him the file. Murli Manohar Joshi was asked to look into the facts. He supported my decision. But it showed to me, how politically sensitive matters can become in Parliament.

Starred questions are listed as such, on the basis of a ballot in which every MP of the House is invited to witness. To avoid any allegation it was decided that instead of manual balloting, it should be done with the help of the computer. Accordingly this method was adopted. However, it was discovered that with this new method, a particular MP, T Subbarami Reddy, was getting starred question listed in his name every day.

Members again complained. The Chairman decided to restore the method of manual balloting. Question Hour is really a sensitive period for all members.

One important development with the potential of creating an interface between Parliament has been the telecasting/ broadcasting of the proceedings of Parliament. The entire Parliamentary proceedings are televised. An important landmark in the history of telecasting of parliamentary proceedings took place in my time on December 14, 2004 when two separate dedicated satellite channels for telecasting nationwide live the proceedings of Rajya Sabha and Lok Sabha were launched by Hon'ble Chairman/Speaker. When televising started in Parliament, it was expected that the members could behave with greater decorum. But exactly the opposite happened. Aware that they were being watched, they became more vociferous in their speeches. Disrupting the House, shouting slogans, coming to the well of the House has become more frequent. It gives the member greater publicity, and members of the constituency admire the activeness of their representative, in Parliament.

I observed another characteristic in the behaviour of the parties. Once there was a demand for laying on the table of the House a report of the CVC. The Congress was demanding it be laid while the BJP was stating that as it is a confidential document, it should not be made public. It was decided that the Chairman should decide. The Chairman consulted the CVC and then gave his finding denying permission for the report to be laid on the table of the House. The Congress silently heard the ruling and then walked out en masse. They boycotted the house for full twelve days till the House was adjourned sine-die on the due date.

The ruling party, the BJP could have easily passed all the bills in the House in the absence of the opposition. But this is where the democratic spirit prevails in the Parliament. No bill was introduced in the House in the absence of the opposition. Only formal business was gone through.

I have also seen the Members of Parliament speaking aggressively in the House, and almost coming to fisticuffs with the members on the other side. I have seen them tearing the papers in the hands of the minister. But as soon as the House adjourns for the day they are seen laughing, cracking jokes, putting their arms around each other's neck. There are no permanent animosities within the House; they obey the instructions and dictates of their whips and party leaders. But outside the House, they remain friends. I then understood the meaning of the concept of "no permanent friends and no permanent enemies".

Humour in Parliament

Mahatma Gandhi had said that humour is both a tranquilliser and equalizer. When the proceedings in the House get monotonous, a witty remark either from the Chair or a member provides a new direction to the debates and discussions. It is said that the most perfect humour and wit are impromptu and unconscious. The exchanges in the House are also neither pre-rehearsed nor pre-meditated, making them thoroughly enjoyable and delightful.

During the course of half-an-hour discussion on a starred question regarding erection of barbed wire fencing along the Indo-Bangladesh border, the following humorous exchanges took place between the Deputy Chairman Dr Najma Heptulla and Sri Jaswant Singh:

Jaswant Singh : Indeed I will attempt to confine myself…

Deputy Chairman : … within the barbed wire fencing. I am just reminding you.

Jaswant Singh : From you Madam Deputy Chairman, the last thing I expected really was the barbed response….

Deputy Chairman : The roses are always accompanied by some thorns.

Jaswant Singh : As long as I have the roses, I will put up with the thorns.

Once when Sri Bhairon Singh was in the Chair during Question Hour, the issue of priority to drought affected states under 'Hariyali' scheme was being taken up. The person raising the question was a member, Sri Balkavi Bairagi, who was a well-known poet. The Chairman requested Bairagi to say something in verse. This is how the humorous banter developed.

Prem Chand Gupta : Sir, Bairagi Sahib has renounced the world, why are you involving him in worldly affairs?

Chairman : It is only because of your company that he is involving himself in worldly affairs, otherwise he would not have been interested in them.

Balkavi Bairagi : Hon'ble Chairman, Sir, I am greatly obliged for your kind words. Honestly it is only because of love (Prem) that I am caught in worldly affairs.

To this the Chairman cautioned: "If it is so because of love, you will be cheated!"

Thus, depending on the Presiding Officer, humour enlivens the proceedings.

Anti-Defection Law and Party Dictatorship

Under the garb of the Anti-Defection Law, the party takes over complete control of the Members of Parliament. It is the party whip who decides which Member will speak; it is the party whip who decides what the Member will speak and for how long. The Chairman is expected to call the speakers in the order advised by the party whip who gives the list to the Secretary-General of the House.

Once a very unique incident took place inside the House. In the Rajya Sabha, Mani Shankar Aiyar, Minister of Panchayati Raj was to answer the starred questions pertaining to his Ministry. The opposition, ie the BJP, was shouting and heckling the minister. The replies given by the minister could not be heard and neither the questions asked. The minister then took the unusual step of going to the member, who was asking the question and answering the question literally, where the member was sitting. If a supplementary question was asked, Mani Shankar would again move from his bench, to where the questioner was sitting and reply, and come back to his seat. This went on for some time till the House was adjourned.

My stay in Parliament gave me a chance to assess how democracy was working in India. A majority of the members are well behaved, intelligent and excellent speakers. They are impressive in their reasoning and logic, and though sometimes, they appear to be outlandish in their behaviour, it is because of the directives given by their party leaders. It is amusing to see the members of the ruling and the opposition parties behaving in the same manner, depending on whether they are in the ruling party or the opposition. Mirror images, I would put it!

In July 2007, elections to fill the offices of the President and Vice-President were held, as the existing incumbents were completing their terms. The Secretary-Generals of the Lok Sabha and Rajya Sabha are returning officers, by rotation, for both these posts. In 2007, I was the Returning Officer for the election of the Vice-President while the Secretary-General of the Lok Sabha was the Returning Officer for the elections to the President of India.

Before the date fixed for receiving the nominations, SS Ahluwalia, MP of the BJP came to see me in my office. He saw a painting of Lord Ganesh adorning my room as well as some other religious artefacts. In a friendly way, he advised me to remove them, during the period of elections. I told him that I had always kept them in my room and I saw no reason to remove them from my room. After he left, I pondered over his advice. Is it that those who will come to file their nominations, and see the painting and religious artefacts, would think of me as a BJP person? Would they think I would be biased in my approach? Would I be thought as non-secular? However I discarded these thoughts as I had supervised and conducted many elections before in my career. If somebody would think about me in this manner, let them do so. Our elections in India are so transparent and open, and the Election Commission is so independent, that no Returning Officer would be able to do anything hanky-panky, least of all in the election of the President and Vice-President of India.

Prime Minister Manmohan Singh and Smt Sonia Gandhi came to file the first set of nominations for Hamid Ansari for Vice-Presidentship. Lalu Prasad Yadavji filed another set of nomination for Sri Hamid Ansari with additional set of proposers. Sometimes later the BJP delegation came to file the nomination of Najma Heptulla. Additional nomination papers were also filed for her with a separate list of proposers. After the two main parties had filed their nomination papers, we also had nominations filed by three other candidates. One candidate came walking backwards. He explained that for some mystical reason he had been walking backward for many years!

On scrutiny only the contestants of the two major parties remained.

The results of the Vice-Presidential elections went decisively in favour of the Congress candidate Sri Hamid Ansari. After declaring him elected, and after informing the Election Commission, I went to Sri Hamid Ansari's house to deliver, and hand over a copy of the declaration. Of course he was immensely happy.

Bhairon Singh Shekhawat contested for the office of the President of India and lost. He told me, much later, that the Congress had offered him the post of Vice-President and had assured him of the party's full support. In turn, they wanted the BJP to support the Congress nominee for Presidentship, Smt Pratibha Patil. However the 'lion' that he was, he had refused. His refusal was also based on the support promised to him orally by Sri Sharad Pawar of the NCP and Sri Mulayam Singh Yadav of the Samajwadi Party. Both of them later backed out. Smt Pratibha Patil, a comparatively unknown figure, became the President of India.

Once a very incident occurred. When Sri Jaswant Singh had become the leader of Opposition in Rajya Sabha, he was invited to give lectures abroad. He wrote a note to the Chairman Rajya Sabha, Bhairon Singhji, that he wanted his PS to accompany him, and wrote that while his own travelling expenses were being taken care of by the organisers of the tour but the cost of travel of his PS should be borne by the Rajya Sabha secretariat.

The proposal was examined in the office. The finance wing of the Secretariat wanted to know whether it was a private visit or an official visit. The file was discussed with the Chairman, and with his approval, a query was accordingly sent under my signatures to Sri Jaswant Singh. Actually Sri Jaswant Singh had been invited to give lectures in his personal capacity, because of his in-depth and intimate knowledge of strategic and defence matters. When Sri Jaswant Singh received the aforesaid query, he blew up and went straight to Sri Shekhawat to complain. The Chairman apparently said nothing as he was already in the know of the whole situation. I was asked to go and apologise to Sri Jaswant Singh. I went straight to his office and sat down in front of him. I said, "I am sorry" hoping that he would say something. He did not say anything. I knew that if I uttered one wrong word, he would catch on and blast me. I maintained a diplomatic silence. He also kept quiet. He kept on looking at me and after a tense five minutes he said, "you may go now." I left promptly and informed Sri Shekhawat that I had apologized!

It was no secret in Rajasthan that Jaswant Singh and Shekhawat were not political friends even though they were in the same party. While Shekhawat supported the Chief Minister Smt Vasundhara Raje Scindia, Jaswant Singh was opposed to her in every way. When Jaswant Singh's son did not get a ticket from the BJP, Jaswant Singh encouraged his son to stand as an independent candidate. This was the last straw and both father and son were expelled from the party.

Another very colourful personality was SS Ahluwalia, a reference of whom, has been made earlier. An astute Parliamentarian, he was the cheer leader of his party. When in opposition, he was the Chief Whip and would be foremost in shouting down the ruling party members or leading his members to the well of the House. When in the ruling party, he would decry the very same antics of the opposition if they entered the well of the House. But at the same time he was very protective of the dignity of the officials of the Secretariat. Once, when an over-enthusiastic member of the BJP, picked up a book from my table and threw it in the air, he reprimanded the member and apologized to me. An experienced practical politician, he was well read, and prepared his speeches and interventions, fully supported by facts. I enjoyed my interactions with him.

I also had the privilege of working closely with Sri Suresh Pachauri, when he was the Minister for Parliamentary Affairs. A young rising political leader, he was well versed in Parliamentary Rules and Regulations. Once, when a particular issue was to be put on the Agenda, for which the Chairman was not in favour, he pressed me late in the evening to have the item included. I tried to contact my Chairman, Sri Shekhawat, but he was not available on the telephone.

I then contacted Smt Sushma Swaraj. She was of the firm view that the item should not be included in the Agenda. However, Sri Pachauri was insistent that as Minister for Parliamentary Affairs, he had the right to have the item included. I again tried to contact the Chairman, but there was no response. I then apprised Smt Sushma Swaraj once again and sought her advice, since she had earlier been the Minister for Parliamentary Affairs, in the NDA regime. She conceded that the Minister for Parliamentary Affairs had a right to have the item included. I accordingly did so and the Agenda of the House was sent for printing very late in the night.

The next day, when the Chairman saw the Agenda, he was unhappy at the inclusion of that particular item. I narrated the entire story of the previous evening. He then called Suresh Pachauri, who confirmed what I had stated. The Chairman, informed Sri Pachauri, that he would not be taking up this item in the House that day. As the Chairman's decision is final in matters pertaining to the House, Sri Pachauri had nothing to say. This showed me another aspect of Parliamentary etiquette. Every member accepts as final, what the Presiding officer decides. That is the convention and nobody challenges the ruling of the Chair.

I served under a very dynamic Deputy Chairperson, Smt Najma Heptulla, when NDA was in power. She had the record of serving as the Deputy Chairperson for the longest period in Parliament. She had also been the first lady Parliamentarian to be the President of the International Parliamentary Union (IPU), which had its headquarters in Geneva. She was a strict disciplinarian and would admonish the members if they misbehaved. However once it so happened that she got very angry with the behaviour of some members, who had come to the well of the House and were shouting slogans. She simply walked out without adjourning the House and retired to her room. All the members came to me asking whether the House had been adjourned, and if so, till what time. I went to her room where she was sitting surrounded by members and simply not speaking to anybody. I walked up to her chair and asked whether the House should be formally adjourned, as she had not announced anything before she walked out. She stated that an announcement may be made, adjourning the House till 4 PM. I accordingly went back to the House and announced, from my official desk, that the House had been adjourned till 4 PM. It was then that Smt Ambika Soni came up to me and said that as the Secretary-General did not have any authority to adjourn the House, the proper way to announce would be to say, "The Deputy Chairman has declared that the House stands adjourned till 4 PM." I went up to the mike once again and announced accordingly to an empty House. This was the first time that such a situation had arisen!

After the UPA came into power, we had Sri Rahman Khan as the Deputy Chairman. He was a very simple person, always smiling. He was an experienced Parliamentarian and very well aware of the House rules. He got very well along with all the members. His smile, and ability to laugh, was his strongest weapon. He was a devout Muslim, keenly interested in protecting Waqf properties. He was made the Chairman of the Waqf Committee, apart from other Committees, and brought about a number of progressive measures for the development of these properties. He was absolutely fair and impartial and was popular in all sections of the House.

Every year we used to have several Parliamentary conferences both in India and abroad. The conference of the International Parliamentary Union used to be once in Geneva and once in any other country. The other international conference was under the auspices of the Commonwealth Parliamentary Union. The Secretary-Generals of the Lok Sabha and the Rajya Sabha always accompanied these delegations apart from an equal number of members from both the Houses. Before we proceeded abroad, all the members of the delegation were given detailed briefing by the officials of the Ministry of External Affairs. Extensive notes were given of the country we were to visit. Except for one or two members, others were not too keen to go through the notes. I found once a lady member also taking her small child with her and spending more time with him, then in the main conference!

Such Parliamentary delegations are always headed by the Speaker. The Deputy Chairman of the Rajya Sabha is invariably a member. While any member is free to speak, I found that except for two or three members, the rest spent their time listening or shopping. The CPI members were usually well-prepared and spoke well.

During the Conferences, the Secretary-Generals meet in their own meetings of the Association of Secretary-Generals. We read our papers on various topics of interest, highlighting the initiatives undertaken in our respective Parliaments. I was privileged to be on the Executive Committee of the Association.

Once we went to Fiji as part of a Parliamentary delegation. I read out my paper "Computerisation in the Parliament of India". Next day, Jaya Prada, the famous actress and Member of Parliament, rushed to show me the daily bulletin, wherein, on the first page was my speech with my photograph. She was as excited as I was. I and Sri Malhotra, Secretary-General of Lok Sabha, took several photographs with her. Sri Somnath Chatterjee, Speaker and leader of our delegation, was equally proud and delighted.

In one of the islands, near Fiji, we were taken for sight-seeing and taste of the ocean air. There, for the first time I saw visitors doing para sailing on top of the sea. I could not resist myself. I quickly bought, one of the local made, coloured Bermudas, enlisted myself, for the para sailing, and was soon soaring in the blue skies above the ocean. It was a thrilling experience. There were plentiful looks of admiration from our MPs, when I landed back on the island.

I met Akhilesh Yadav, for the first time, when we went for the IPU meeting in Geneva. He was intelligent, youthful looking and always smiling. I carried a very favourable impression about him. When I met him later, in Lucknow, he had become the Chief Minister of Uttar Pradesh, and I had retired. However, he still vividly remembered our first meeting in Geneva.

I must also mention another member, who became a good friend of mine. Dinesh Trivedi, who later became the Railway Minister for a short while, had a unique sense of humour. Both of us used to crack jokes. He was positive minded, with a modern outlook, and well read. I got on very well with him, as we also shared a common friend, Avinash Sahai of Calcutta, who had been my class-fellow in school. Our jokes were a bit raunchy. He fell out of favour with Mamata Banerjee, his party leader, as he had taken some very bold steps for reforming the financial position of the Railways, which were in tune with the thinking of Prime Minister Manmohan Singh, but out of sync with the policies of Mamata Banerjee. He had to resign, though the intelligentsia of the nation was behind him.

Another person I cannot forget is Hema Malini, who was initially a nominated member, but later joined the BJP. A charming personality, she was easily the most beautiful member in the House. She was an active member and was asked to speak on several issues by her party. As she was from Tamil Nadu, she used to speak in Hindi in a very sweet manner. I remember an incident in Geneva, when we were all having breakfast together with the leader of our delegation, Sri Somnath Chatterjee. Various issues of the country were being discussed including the conditions in Bengal. Suddenly Hema Malini in her innocent voice said in Hindi, *"Bengali log kam bahut kam karte hai, par bolte bahut hai"* (Bengalis work very little, but speak a lot). Everybody was stunned, specially the Speaker Sri Somnath Chatterjee, who hailed from Bengal. He was nonplussed for a moment but gathered himself and sportingly admitted that this was the general perception of Bengal all over India, though it was not true. We all suppressed our laughter.

Sri Somnath Chatterjee was an outstanding person, but he naturally had a special love for Bengal as well as Bengalis. Sourav Ganguly was the captain of the Indian cricket team and was performing brilliantly. Whenever he scored a century or won the Test matches a special mention was made in both houses of his performances. The special mention was always made first in the Lok Sabha and we followed suit, so as not be left behind. Sri Somnath Chatterjee was so unassuming that when my daughter got married in Delhi, even though I could not get time to meet him and invite him personally, he came and blessed my daughter. Together with my Chairman Shekhawat, he spent one hour meeting all the guests. One of the guests was Sanjeev Ahluwalia, who was then Joint Secretary, Disinvestment in the Government of India. When, Somnath Chatterjee asked him as to how the work of the Department was proceeding, Sanjeev mischievously told him, "Sir, you are not allowing us to work," referring to the opposition of the Communist Party to disinvestment. Somnath Chatterjee broke into a loud guffaw and went on laughing to the amusement of all the *baratis*!

Brinda Karat was another member whom I respected. She was always well-prepared and gave brilliant speeches. Like Sitaram Yechury, of her party, all statements she made were supported by logical arguments. She was always simply dressed and yet retained her charm. Sitaram Yechury was an excellent orator. He was unique in the way he spoke. There was no bitterness or rancour in his speeches. He marshalled his facts well and was always disciplined. I have never seen him coming to the well of the House.

Jaya Bhaduri was another active member. She always attended the sittings of the House and would stay the full day. She spoke eloquently with facts and figures. However she was disqualified once from membership for holding an office of profit in Uttar Pradesh. She came back four months later. I had a special relationship with her, as her husband Amitabh Bachchan was from the same Boys High School, Allahabad, as I was.

When the UPA came back to power in 2004, it was discovered that many of the members were holding offices of profit which made them liable for disqualification under the Disqualification of Members Act. This included members mainly from the ruling party and its supporting groups. Sonia Gandhi, as Chairman of the NAC was also one of the members who could have been affected. Therefore the UPA Government decided to make an amendment to the Act and exclude those posts from the ambit of disqualification. The Bill was passed in both the Houses and went to the President for assent. After some days, the President sent the Bill back to Parliament for reconsideration on certain specific points. His communication to the House was:

1. I received on 25th May 2006, the Parliament (Prevention of Disqualification) Amendment Bill 2006, duly passed

by both Houses of Parliament for my assent under Article 111 of the Constitution of India.

2. While having the highest regard for the sagacity and mature wisdom of Parliamentarians and with due deference to the Parliament, I would like the Parliament to reconsider the proposed Bill:

   (a) in the context of the settled interpretation of the expression 'Office of Profit' in Article 102 of the Constitution, and

   (b) the underlying Constitutional principles therein.

3. While reconsidering, among other things, the following may be specifically addressed:

   1. Evolution of generic and comprehensive criteria which are just, fair and reasonable and can be applied across all States and Union territories in a clear and transparent manner.

   2. The implication of including for exemption the names of offices the holding of which is alleged to disqualify a member and in relation to which petitions for disqualifications are already under process by the competent authority.

   3. Soundness and propriety of law in making the applicability of the amendment retrospectively.

   4. As provided under Article 111 of the Constitution, I, therefore hereby return the Bill to the Houses for reconsideration with this message.

However since the UPA had a majority in both the Houses, Parliament again passed the Bill and sent it back to the President for his assent. President Kalam, acting constitutionally, thereafter gave his assent immediately. At the same time the ruling parties appeared quite unhappy with the President as they felt that delay in giving assent was because of BJP pressures on the President.

Another interesting incident I remember was that of Shibu Soren. He was a Member of Parliament but was absconding in a murder case registered against him. One day he was noticed by some members inside the Rajya Sabha precincts. The opposition members began shouting, "Arrest him, arrest him," as he scampered away. Under the rules no police is allowed inside, but as they saw him running away, they all had a good laugh.

The House has its moments of laughter and fun. Once a very aged member of the House, Sri Goenka, asked a question on the dancing girls of Mumbai. As he rose to ask his supplementary, Chairman Shekhawat looked at him, and said "Mr Goenka at your age what is your interest in dancing girls?" Goenka rose and said, "Sir, you and I are both in the same condition." The entire House had a hearty laugh.

Lalu Prasad could always bring the house down with his witticisms. His humour is unique as he speaks in his Bihari style. When he was the Minister for Railways, he would reply to his detractors with repartees that not only showed his depth of knowledge of his Ministry but also shut up the questioner.

Shekhawat was also very strict on the members, especially if he found anyone indulging in unethical behaviour. Once a member from Muzaffarnagar asked a question which was listed for oral answer. When the question was put up, the member was absent. The question related to a particular industry and Shekhawat felt that the member had been 'persuaded' not to ask the question. Next day the member was reprimanded by the Chairman and he was hard put to explain his absence (and innocence)!

When Sri Somnath Chatterjee took the initiative in starting the Lok Sabha TV, he sent a letter to the Chairman Shekhawat, inviting Rajya Sabha to also join in the venture. The proposal was discussed in the General Purposes Committee of the Rajya Sabha. There was a vociferous opposition from Smt Sushma Swaraj and other BJP members as there was no role for the members of the Rajya Sabha in the running of the Parliamentary channel which was still to be called the Lok Sabha TV. In the in-house examination of the proposal, I recommended that at this stage, we should join and participate in the setting up of the channel, and then later we can set up our own Rajya Sabha TV based on the experienced gained. But because of the decision in the General Purpose Committee, the proposal was not approved.

Some weeks later, our Deputy Chairman Sri Rahman Khan told me that when he was discussing the TV proposal with Sri Somnath Chatterjee, the latter informed him that the proposal was shot down in the Rajya Sabha because Yogendra Narain, Secretary-General, Rajya Sabha had opposed it. I was shocked. I showed the file to Sri Rahman Khan and also my recommendations. He read the entire noting and then clarified the matter with Somnath Chatterjee. The misunderstanding was cleared. But I realized that somebody had deliberately created this wrong impression in the Speaker's mind.

In Parliament there is always a shortage of rooms. It is the Lok Sabha Secretariat, under the Speaker, which decides which rooms should be allotted to the Rajya Sabha Secretariat officials and their Committees and which should be allotted for the officials, staff and Committees of the Lok Sabha. We in the Rajya Sabha always felt that we were being discriminated against. Even when the additions to the Parliament Annexe were made, we were not given any additional allotments. In the several meetings held with the Secretary-General Lok Sabha, I requested him to show under which authority or orders, the Lok Sabha has taken upon itself the power to allot the rooms in Parliament. They could never show these orders. They simply stated that by convention, the Speaker of the Lok Sabha has the control of the building and lands belonging to Parliament or within its precincts. As neither the Chairman nor I wanted to challenge the powers of the Speaker, we preferred to close the matter.

The President addresses Parliament every year at the beginning of the Budget session. The joint session is held in the Central Hall. The practice was, that the President reads his speech in English and the Vice-President, reads a complete translation of the speech in Hindi. One year, while reading the translated speech, Shekhawat fainted, and almost fell. His personal staff supported him as he sat down. The President declared the Hindi speech as read and after observing due formalities, closed the joint session.

Since then the practice of reading the translated speech has been confined to the reading of the opening and closing paragraph.

During the President's speech no member is expected to shout slogans or show any disrespect to the President. But occasionally even this convention is sometimes flouted.

The Central Hall is the place where all Parliamentarians, ex-Parliamentarians, state legislators meet and interact. Accredited journalists are also permitted and they pick up interesting bytes from the members.

Parliamentarians usually have their lunch in the Parliament canteens as it is very cheap. Catering is done by the Railways and large amounts of subsidy is given both by the Lok Sabha and

Rajya Sabha secretariats to the Railways to enable serving of food at cheap rates. I do not find anything objectionable in this because buying food from the market every day will be expensive, time consuming and unhealthy for the members. However the subsidy could be certainly reduced.

Journalists, recognized by the respective Secretariats, are provided a separate enclosure in the galleries reserved for the visitors. Few people realise the important role journalists play in providing coverage to the Parliamentary proceedings. Apart from the live TV broadcast there is no other medium, except the newspapers, by which the citizens can know what is happening in Parliament. In fact, if the journalists report incorrectly, they can face contempt. If the Speaker or any other Presiding officer, expunge some words or sentences from the proceedings, the journalists are barred from reporting these portions in the newspapers.

In India, the provision of punishment for contempt of Parliament still exists. Originally, we borrowed this concept from the British Parliament, but while the mother of all Parliaments, has given up this privilege, we in India are still clinging to it. We are just not willing to give up this privilege. It is interesting to know that our Constitution had originally included an Article which stated that the privileges of Parliament would be the same as that of the British Parliament. Later on, in the mid-seventies, the Article was amended to say that the privileges of Parliament would be the same as they stood when the Constitution was adopted. The word 'British' was removed.

The Parliamentarians are also unwilling to enact legislation to codify the law relating to contempt of Parliament including the quantum of punishment. The logic given is, that if it is codified, it will become justiciable and be amenable to appeal in courts and interpretation by the judiciary. Parliament would not like to like to let go of its sovereignty and exclusiveness in this regard.

As far as the funding of Parliament is concerned, both the Houses of Parliament, individually prepare their budgets for the year, and after getting it approved from the respective Presiding Officers, send them for concurrence of the Finance Department. Apart from a few queries, the conventional practice is, that the Finance Department agrees in toto with the prepared estimates. Parliament is therefore never in shortage of funds. If additional funds are required, they are promptly provided.

Often a demand is raised in the public and the press that when Parliament does not function, then the parliamentarians should not be paid their daily honorarium. This has never been accepted as the ruling party will always accuse the opposition for disrupting the House, and that they should not be penalized for the acts of the opposition. The present practice is, that a member, as soon as he is about to enter the House, signs an attendance register. After that, whether he stays for the full day, half day or not at all, he will be paid his daily allowance. As Parliamentarians decide their own pay and allowances, it will be difficult to approve of any such penal provision.

Certain other reforms have been attempted. For example to prevent disruption of Question Hour, the Chairman Rajya Sabha Sri Hamid Ansari moved the Question Hour from 11 AM to the afternoon. But the members were not happy and it was reverted back to 11 AM. The Chairman has again changed it back to the afternoon. There is an inherent resistance to change in the Parliamentarians.

Nobody can reform Parliament, except the Parliamentarians themselves. Public pressure, media pressure and constituency pressure can bring out the desired change. But even this pressure has to be consistently put on all the major political parties, both at the Centre and the States, and not only on the ruling parties. At present this obstructionism and shouting, has been accepted as a part of democratic functioning. Unfortunately this is a worldwide phenomenon, as we saw, when we witnessed the functioning of the European Parliament.

No political party should get the feeling that having won the elections, they have acquired the license to run the country and Parliament, as they like arbitrarily. They must understand that they have been given the reins of office to steer the country on the path of development and growth, taking the people along with them. They are responsible to the citizens who have elected them.

'In Democracy We Trust' should be the motto of all political parties.

Chapter 10

General Reflections on the State of the Nation

APART from over population and abject poverty in the rural areas, we also have a high rate of unemployment.

We do not have a policy of giving doles or monthly support to those whose income is below the poverty line. The western armchair economists would scoff at the idea of spending money on such doles, but, on the other hand, press for lower taxation on the incomes of those, who are already rich. They promote the idea of generation of wealth amongst those who are already rich. For those, who are poor, the economists would prefer schemes, which incrementally increase their incomes, like the National Rural Employment Guarantee Scheme or the Gram Sadak Yojana etc. Even for implementing these schemes there is no trained manpower, and thus leakages occur, which diverts the money flow, to the powerful and the rich.

Why can't we ensure providing the poor with financial resources equal to the difference between the country's per capita income and their actual income. Each citizen must actually get the per capita income as the minimum income. In the telecom sector, the government charges a certain amount from each licensee, which goes into the Universal Obligation

Fund. From this Fund, the government implements its avowed policy of developing the mobile services in the rural areas. On similar lines, we can build up a Poverty Fund, based and funded by a certain percentage of the Income Tax, payable by persons earning, let us say, above ₹ 10 lakh a year and use this Fund for distributing 'Poverty Coupons' to those living below the poverty line or for running subsidized kitchens like the 'Amma's Kitchen' in Tamil Nadu.

In my experience of administration in different districts, I was often perplexed, by the sight of individuals, begging on the streets, with weak, wrinkled up bodies with barely any clothes, sitting under the trees, or boys and girls wearing torn clothes moving about in the villages or in the urban slums. I used to feel helpless and guilty. Being a representative of the government, I was haunted with the feeling of being unable to do anything for them. It was not only a question of giving them money – it was a realization of guilt.

A question often came to my mind, as to whether the law, only protects certain vested interests who are in power. Can therefore, law, be said to be biased in favour of the powerful classes and groups that made the law. For example, law gives protection to the rich and the assets of the rich, in form of properties, money, other financial assets, their industries, factories etcetera. On the other hand what does it give to the poor and the landless? In India, there is no social cover for the poor, the old and the ill and those who are starving. It does not ensure food to the hungry.

India has consciously not adopted the Chinese model of absolute government, India has a Constitution which guarantees various freedoms, including the freedom of speech, the freedom of the press, freedom of movement and equality before the law. We pride ourselves in stating that our democracy is a liberal democracy. However, these freedoms, enshrined in our Constitution, also become a reason for weak governance, as compared to China. Even though we are rated as the fastest growing economy in the world, our GDP is only 1,177 billion dollars while the GDP of China is 3,206 billion dollars. While our annual growth was 10.2% between 2002-2007 the Chinese growth rate was 13.7% for the same period. On the other hand the decline in the growth of the manufacturing sector in India has resulted in the Service sector contributing up to 60% of our GDP while in China it is only 40.4%. The unemployment percentage figure for China in 2007 was 4% while in India it was 8%.

Many people link the policies followed during the Emergency, with that of China. They still talk about the beneficial effect of the Emergency, on the working culture of the people. It would be ridiculous to dismiss these ideas as completely wrong. Perhaps, in many aspects, government should be feared, though not like China, in all aspects. Fear can make you obey and become more disciplined, but on the other hand, it prevents you from unleashing your full potential. We would still like to see our artists, writers, industrialists, agriculturalists, computer scientists unleash their full energies, and make their mark, in the areas they are working in. We must also encourage the spirit of toleration, as that is an essential ingredient in any democracy.

We may not appreciate certain aspects of MF Husain's painting, but still, will not tolerate the violent attack on him and his exhibits. Most of us felt unhappy, when he was forced to leave India and take the citizenship of another country. Many of us, may not like the writing of Bangladeshi writer Taslima Nasrin, who has sought refuge in India, because of her so-called 'blasphemous' writings, but we would still like her visa to be extended from time to time, to enable her to continue with her creative writing. We may not like everything what the Press writes in India or what is shown on TV, but we would all vehemently resist any State censorship, like in China. There is a difference in our cultural heritage and learning. It might be, though we may not admit it, because of the British rule in India which exposed the Indian people to the ideas of liberty, equality and social justice. The writings of the Fabian Socialists of UK, and the political philosophy of Bentham. Locke and Rousseau, influenced our Constitution makers, who had all received English education. Therefore any idea of an absolute State is anathema to us. But perhaps we need to follow a Middle Path, the path which our greatest legacy to the world, Buddhism teaches. A mixture of the two philosophies the liberal and the autocratic – make a good concoction.

I found in my administrative career that administration is too paternal. The politicians and the administrators at the top, decide what the people need, and in what manner it should be doled out to them. It seems to be the legacy, we inherited, in the era of our strong friendship with Russia, when we adopted Central planning, as a national strategy and set up a Planning Commission to not only identify the deficiencies and short falls in the area of development including industry, agriculture, infrastructure, services but also left it to the same Planning Commission, to do micro planning, to ensure that money goes into those activities, which have been identified by our planners, administrators and economists sitting in the Planning Commission. How many kilometres of village road have to be constructed, which villages are to be connected to the main district roads, and national highways, what type of loans are to be given to those, who do not have houses, what should be the strategy for providing irrigation facilities, how many schools are to be set up, how many Primary Health Centres are to be set up and where, etc, is left to the Central and State Planning Commission.

Planning at the top level has the disadvantage, that it is not demand oriented. When one plans for the entire country, it becomes necessary to set up an impartial criteria and those executing the schemes, at the field level, have to fall in line. We will thus have Primary Health Centres, where no such demand exists; we will have homes in villages under the Indira Awaas Yojana built with designs, which are not suitable to the local people; schools will be set up in remote areas where neither students, nor teachers would go. It would be better to merely earmark funds for various sectors, and leave it to the State and district agencies to execute them in the manner they think best based on advise given by civil society, at the field level. India is a vast big country and civil society should be more involved at the field level. While the Central Planning Commission (now NITI Aayog) and the State Planning Commissions, may be directly involved in schemes above a certain financial level (say ₹ 1,000 crore and above for the Centre and ₹ 500 crore at the State level), the rest of the development schemes should be developed and executed by the district level authorities.

This will of course necessitate capacity building at the field level. The concept of Block Development Officers was introduced in India almost five decades back. But they are not a professional body of development executives. The professional training required to make them development executives is missing. They have become general administrators and are unable to provide leadership in the rural areas. We need to develop a rural administrative service and train the personnel so recruited, to work as Secretaries in the Village Panchayat, as Block Development Officers, or as Chief

Executive Officers of the Zila Parishad. It should be a rural oriented service, with a mandate of working in the rural areas only. They should not be moved out to urban areas and should have the same status as the IAS. It is surprising that though we repeatedly say that 60% of our people live in rural areas yet those who carry out the administration in the rural areas, whether they are Tehsildars, Block Development Officers, Village Lekhpals or Panchayat Secretaries, are a neglected lot and their status made subordinate to the officers serving in urban areas. Like the IAS, there should be various grades and promotions of the officers of a new IAS (Rural) service. They should start as Panchayat Secretaries, get training in all the departments, operating in the rural areas, and move up as Block Development Officers, Naib Tehsildars, Tehsildars and Sub-Divisional Officers (SDOs). Time has come when we should set up this service immediately otherwise the rural areas will continue to remain neglected, and a drag on the national economy in health, education, and infrastructure.

What is the difference between the government and those who are governed? The government is elected by those who are governed. After sometime, if those, who have been elected lose, new governors come in power and the former governors became part of the governed. Why do people want to become governors of the public? Is it the lure of power, the opportunity to lord over others or is it the opportunity to serve, to make the nation more powerful, and the people more prosperous? Are political parties formed, because, members of each party genuinely have difference over the policies to be adopted, to make the people and the nation more happy and prosperous? The only method by which the differences, if any in policies can be found out, is through their manifestos. These are documents, produced by the think tanks of each party, professing to declare objectives, for which the party has been formed and the policies they will follow, if they are elected. These manifestos are released with great fanfare and then are buried from the public eyes, once the elections are over. Neither the press, nor the civil society cares to examine the performance of the political party which has come into power, with the manifesto issued by the ruling party. This is one of the greatest democratic frauds – people are promised something and then these promises are forgotten. The individual citizen is not much concerned. He is more concerned, at least in a developing country, with earning his daily bread. His life is occupied either, in looking after his agricultural crops in the rural areas, or going to and fro to his office in the urban areas. Politics does not bother him. Politicians sometime do. For getting votes the politicians may try to influence the local administrator to do something, which is against the law or which will hurt the ordinary non-political citizen. The politician at the local level does not have an objective of cleaning the environment for conducive living. He might however take the help of anti-social elements, the moneyed class, or the local toughies, with the objective of getting votes. Getting votes is the objective – everything, including the welfare of the citizens, is secondary.

How do we eliminate such thinking, in those, whom we elect. Perhaps the best way would be to make them conscious of their performance and of the opinion their constituency carries of them. This is where civil society and media can join hands. In the USA it is being done even now. Every year surveys are carried out as to how the legislators are viewed in their constituency. These surveys are then highlighted by the media to create a public opinion, favourable or unfavourable, on the working of the elected representatives. It is expected that by doing so the legislator will improve his performance.

The survey has to be necessarily done by an identified creditable agency, which, through its impartiality, can be depended to help the citizens in making an independent judgement of working of the legislator. It would also help if, a factual report based on certain pre-meditated factors, is the basis for giving an opinion. It could be for example:

1. The roads which have been built in his constituency (name wise).
2. The primary, secondary and high schools which he has helped to establish (location wise).
3. The number of tube wells he has been able to install in the rural areas of his constituency (village wise).
4. The number of self-help groups which he has helped to form in his time.
5. The number of small and large industries he has been able to establish in his constituency.
6. The names of villages/slum areas he has visited during his tenure with details of what he could do for their improvement.
7. The number of houses electrified in his constituency during his time.
8. The days he participated in the proceedings of the legislature, and so on.

If such factual reports are published it would help to motivate the legislator to improve his performance. Democracy would get strengthened, and there would be a greater bonding between the legislator and his constituency. Today, unfortunately the prestige and power of the legislator is somehow linked to how many times he has been able to get his District Magistrate and Superintendent of Police transferred, the number of

Thanedars (police SHOs)who listen to him and do his bidding etc. The legislator of the ruling party always holds an upper hand in such matter and therein lies his clout. An answer to this problem could be that the terms of the District Magistrate should be co-terminus with that of the government. Like the legislator, who gets elected for a fixed term and who cannot be removed except as laid down in the Constitution and Parliamentary rules, the district officials and the Secretaries to the government should be similarly made non-transferable for the same period. If the official does something against the law or is acting illegally, then let the law take its own course. Elected representative should be barred, either by law or by convention, in recommending transfers and postings of officials. Such recommendations may also be treated as unethical behaviour by a member of the legislature. They can certainly make complaints against the officials, which should be enquired into, not politically, but by a committee of persons consisting of the three senior most civil servants of the State or the Centre as the case may be (of the government concerned). This would be on the lines of the judiciary. Punishment, or appropriate administrative disciplinary actions, should follow the recommendations of the Committee.

It is unfortunate that while the judiciary can punish people for its contempt and the legislatures can punish for contempt, the executive has no such powers. Why is this so? There is no explanation in political science literature. If we accept the fact, that in a democracy, we have to give impartial administration, treating each person equally, then administration should be left free of the political executive. The argument against this is that in a parliamentary democracy the executive is responsible to the legislature and therefore the executive cannot be left unfettered. But here we must distinguish between the executive and the administration. While the political executive can be, and should be, responsible to the legislature, and answer all the queries of the legislature, on matters of policy, day to day administration cannot be subjected to legislative control. Administration, conceptually has to be separated from the political executive, whose duty should be, to lay down overall policies and a broad policy control over the executive. The political executives should retain overall control over the Ministry, but the officers, working in the Ministry, or the Secretariat, should be left under the control of their Secretary, Additional Secretary and Joint Secretary, etc, who are there to assist the ministers. Similarly the departmental heads in the field, who are meant to execute and implement the policies laid down by the Ministries, can be broadly under the control of the Ministry but 'a hands off' policy should be adopted on their day to day decision-making.

A very pertinent question that arises in governance is, why people accept the political and administrative system without even knowing fully about it. Is it that the human tendency is to accept the existing environment without questioning it? Most of the citizens would not have heard of political philosophers like Bentham, or Rousseau or terms like the Social Contract, which is at the back of the concept of a republican government. They would not even have heard of John Stuart Mill and the Bill of Rights. They would not have heard of the concept of the General Will. Why then, do we just enter a political eco-system and mentally submit ourselves to it? Do we have the right to rebel against the system we are born in?

An answer to this would be found perhaps in the Nature of man. Human beings love harmony and would do the least to disturb it. If mentally, man is in harmony with the system, or has found nothing wrong enough to make him resist or overthrow it, he will be in favour of the Status Quo. We never knew who the Constitution makers were, except their names and biographic details. We do not know how they assumed they were representing all the people living at that time and those unborn, when they prepared to enact the Constitution on behalf of "We the people of India". Even if we can be made to believe that they were some sort of representatives of the people of India, living in that particular period, can they bind down the future citizens of India to all those principles which they felt were necessary at that time. The first proof of the fallacy of this assumption was the legislation relating to abolition of Zamindari which was struck down by the apex court as being contrary to the principle of right to own property as given in the Constitution. The Constitution had to be amended to include Schedule IX to protect land reform legislations, which were necessitated by the policies adopted by those in power.

Is the Constitution then, subject to change, like any other organization? Like a toddler grows up to be a boy, a boy into man, a man into senior citizen, does the Constitution of a country have to keep on modifying itself, though the soul remains the same? Our Constitution itself prescribes the procedure as to how it can be amended, and so long as we follow the procedure, we are permitted to do so. It also prescribes, how the individual freedoms granted by it, can be temporarily suspended at times of emergency. The government of the day, elected, by due process, as prescribed in the Constitution and having a majority in Parliament can turn the Constitution up side down, following Constitutional procedures. Its interpretation of emergency clauses can be vigorously defended before the judiciary, and depending on the majority of the judges, the nation can be subjected to arbitrary action. Did we, the people of India really give all these powers to our elected representatives? The reality is, that our Constitution framers, considered the Government of India Act 1935 as their basic document (enacted by the British Government for their colony, India) and then added certain new chapters and clauses to make it suitable for a new democratic nation, yet to be born. The inclusion of Fundamental Rights, individual freedoms and Directive Principles of State Policy were welcomed. But the colonial limitations inbuilt in the Constitution, were a regressive feature. Declaration of Emergency, and the right to take over the governance of a province by suspending the State legislature, were appropriate for a government, administering a colony, but not for a nation which had made a tryst with destiny and was eager to 'redeem its pledge'. The anti-democratic provisions of the Constitution were certainly not the contribution of our Constitution framers, but the left-overs of the Government of India Act 1935, which we left untouched, like many other provisions of the aforesaid Act.

This was symbolic of the thinking of our Constitution makers, who found the Constitution of the British system of administration, as suitable, for the stability of the country. The much despised civil service, which had helped the perpetuation of the British rule, was also to continue. What was good for the British would be good for independent India. The Constitution framers were mostly the product of the British educational system, and obviously saw much good in it. It was a wise step in many ways, but it also helped in perpetuating the colonial mind set. The District Magistrate continued to be the *'mai-bap'* of the populace under his jurisdiction. He disposed justice, according to the British (Indian) Penal Code, British (Indian) Criminal Procedure Code, and the British (Indian)

Evidence Act. To be fair, the Criminal justice system in India had been well-tested and tried over time and found to meet our needs. The British had left an efficient judicial system, which was however supported by an extremely colonial minded police set up. The police, under the British, had been quite ruthless. They were a corrupt force, but were well protected by the British, as the police could help in identifying not only the bad elements, but also the freedom fighters, who were a threat to the British. The British built up a very efficient intelligence gathering system, and our elected post independent politicians found that this system, served their needs also. While earlier, the intelligence agencies, used to keep a watch on the Indian Freedom Fighters, who were a threat to the British, the present day politicians in powers found the system effective in keeping a track of their political opponents. During Elections, the intelligence agencies are also used by the governments in power, to find out how many seats can be won by the ruling parties, who are the influential persons in a constituency, who can swing votes in their favour etc. As far as governance was concerned, the ruling party merely put themselves, in the shoes of the British, and perpetuated the colonial mentality, including putting down their political opponents, by lodging false cases and arresting them with the help of the police.

This perpetuation of the colonial policies, however, had a negative effect in more ways then one. It perpetuated, for example, corruption. The police, well-protected by the politicians in power, asserted themselves, almost becoming extortionist in the process. While the Superintendents of Police were well read, educated and constituted the IPS, the Thanedars continued to be of the same brutal mentality. Pay or be put in jail. False witnesses are the order of the day. Brutal beating up of people kept in lock ups, without trial. Money being extorted from the people for routine activities like police verification, passport certification etc. Even investigation of cases is subject to money power.

The other side of the picture is also true. The police at the field level, especially in rural areas, is never adequately funded. Jeeps have been certainly given but not enough money for the petrol. So if the Station House Officer gets a complaint, he first asks the complainant to fill up enough petrol in his jeep, and then the investigation starts. Similarly there is not enough paper even to write the First Investigation Report. The government stationery does not come in the requisite quantity, and so the local shopkeepers, and the local business men are asked to chip in money to provide for the stationery. Several senior officers come for inspection in the *thanas* and all have to be given tea, biscuits, sweets, namkeens etc. Where does the money come from? The funds are collected by the constables, in the *thana* through 'services' rendered to the general populace. These funds are then pooled for common expenditure of the *thana*, like entertainment of superiors, or sometimes for fulfilment of the financial demands of the senior and middle level officers. That is why sometimes allegations are made of the *thanas* being auctioned in the highest bidder. While this is not true in most of the cases, yet in some cases it is a fact.

The pay scales of the lower rungs of both the police and revenue administration are woefully inadequate. Perhaps the colonial administration, in the time of the British wanted to keep it that way, and leave the remaining amount to come out of the local people. The British, never, really fought against the corruption in the lower ranks of the administration. That is why the police today, out of all the branches of administration, have remained as colonial in its nature, as before. They also keep the local politicians of the ruling party well satisfied, so as to avoid transfers. Transfers of field officers usually occur when the local politician of the ruling party gets annoyed. They are more political, then administrative, in nature. That is the main reason why in the States, the average posting of police officers and SHOs is six months to one year. Administration therefore tends to collapse, as every SHO/DSP tends to remain passive where politicians of the ruling party are involved. There is, in short, no equality before the law as actually practised, by the policeman in the field.

What can we do to change the system? There are two solutions to this problem. One is to make the police independent of the political bosses, making it responsible only to its own departmental bosses, i e the DG of Police. The DGP should be a non-transferable post, with a fixed tenure. Once appointed he should not be removed, till the government of the State changes, and should continue for the full term of the government. In addition, the performance of the Superintendent of Police should be assessed by the minister in-charge of the district. In many States, we have ministers in-charge of separate districts of the State. Only such a minister would be competent to recommend transfer of the Superintendent of Police. This would also bring some stability in the system, as Police would only be accountable for their performance to one person at the local level. As a disciplined force, the police should function under its own peers, and not have to look around for political support. Politicians should be kept away from the day to day administration.

A training system for legislators should be set up where, *inter alia*, the elected representatives are made aware of the functioning of administration including the hierarchy of the administrative set up. They should be also made aware of the Constitution and its provisions, as well as the working of the civil service systems.

It is surprising indeed, that our law makers, who come fresh, after winning the elections (in which no educational qualifications are laid down) get a very cursory training (if at all) of only two to three days as how to become effective legislators. Some States do not even have the short-term training period. While in the two other branches of the State, ie the judiciary and the executive, the new incumbents are trained both initially as well as during the long period of the service, to become effective professionals, it is surprising that the legislatures have not yet carved a well thought out training policy for their legislators. A legislator functions, not only within the legislature, but also outside it. As a representative of the people, he also enjoys a unique status in society. People call on him or welcome him to their areas, highlighting their grievances and look forward to a speedy redressal of the same. Does a legislator know how to respond to such demands? Does he know how he should address the officers? Are there any conventions he should obey in dealing with the junior and senior civil servants? If there are any recommendations he has to make on transfers and postings, whom shall he address them to? There are so many other issues which require an awareness in the legislator. A legislator today is not only a lawmaker, he represents democracy before the public – he is the person who can make or unmake the faith of the people in a democracy. He can cause riots by his fiery speeches and he can bring harmony and peace in the neighbourhood, through the influence he exercises, in his constituency.

If the legislator is responsible, he will also act as the eyes and ears of the government. By giving practical suggestions from the field, he can help in modifying strategies, which could enable a policy to be more effective. He can prevent riots from taking place, by his advice, and by his timely information to the administration. He can act as a conduit between the administration and the people, at times of curfew or when there is a credibility gap between the two. In times of war, he can help in mobilization of men and resources. With his speeches, he can raise the morale of the people, and bring the people to the aid of the defence forces. In border areas, he can give the leadership to help the wounded, or to carry messages and local supplies.

With such an important role to perform, does not the legislator need training? A legislator is no ordinary person. He enjoys a number of facilities and privileges to make him perform these functions effectively. He must be trained, to make optimum use of the same. A legislator should make himself a person who is to be admired and emulated. In many ways he represents the government while the civil servant is only an executive authority. But respect, a legislator must learn, cannot be commanded. It has to be earned by proper behaviour, conduct and appropriate use of the powers he possesses. It is neither good for democracy, nor for the legislator, when people look upon him as a predator who only uses his power to make money. Many legislators, who use muscle power to fight elections, end up by becoming stooges of the same people. Politics is a vicious circle. Many politicians rationalize their conduct by saying that the party has directed them to act in a particular manner. The party has asked them to *gherao*, burn buses, lead mobs to vandalize shops, which remain open, in spite of a *bandh*. This has let them do reprehensible activities like destroying paintings of MF Husain (in spite of his worldwide reputation as a famous artist), to break window panes of shops selling Valentine Cards (imposition of cultural values by one set of people against the others), shout slogans and prevent people from expressing their views if they are contrary to the views they or their party holds. In West Bengal it is a frequent sight to see even government-sponsored *bandhs*. This is a new phenomenon. The legislators and party members of the ruling party forcibly close shops, prevent public transport from running, cause inconvenience to the people, and the police stands by quietly, as silent spectators. Where is the rule of law? However, if an opposition party was to do the same, there would be a lathi-charge, even firing, strong criticism by the government, followed by registration of FIRs and arrest.

This has raised a relevant question in the minds of the civil servant as well as in the citizens Is law the handmaid of the government in power? What is the role of the State and the relevance of the Constitution? Can the enforcers of law themselves became the violators of law, and can nothing be done about it. And if the law makers are free to break the law, what moral right do they have to order the arrest of ordinary people, who do the very same thing.

Similarly, a politician is often seen in company of people who are not looked upon well in society. Either they are the local goondas, extortionists, blackmailers, smugglers or gamblers and tax evaders. Legislators must be advised by their party leaders to avoid such people. There is a system in the government, whereby names of people, with whom the civil servants should not mix with, are circulated confidentially. There should be a similar system for the legislators, who would be, unknowingly, dealing with them. The legislators must realize that they are as much representatives of the State, as ministers, judges and the civil servants.

The legislators must also be trained in dealing with the media. When important events take place, the legislators are often asked for their reaction. While the party headquarters takes care of the view point of the party, the legislator is often asked the same for local incidents. He should know what to say, otherwise a wrong statement or even an inappropriately worded statement, can create an abnormal situation, making it tough for the district administration to control. The government, as part of its public relation strategy, must also keep the legislators informed of all the programmes and projects being carried out in the districts. This function can also be performed locally by the district officials. It will be useful, both to the legislators, as well as the government. Once the legislator is aware of the programmes he can ensure that these programmes are also extended to the uncovered areas. To the district officials, who want to genuinely know about the impact of these programmes, it will be useful to get a feedback from the legislators, as to how the programmes are running in the field. Bureaucracy cannot and should not, depend on the report of only its subordinate officials, because such official report can be, often, quite biased. It always better to get independent feedbacks, which can help in modifying strategies for implementation of these programmes.

This also bring to the forefront, the role of NGOs. Can NGOs be effective in ensuring good governance? Whom do they represent? Do they represent civil society? These are some of the questions which bother the government as well as the executive administrators in the field. To organize an NGO, either the promoter should have enough money of his own like Bill Gates, or one should be able to attract funding, by the very nature of activities being undertaken by the NGO. On the other hand many NGOs (most of them) depend heavily on government funding for continuing their activities. Others manage to get enough funds initially from the government, or the private sector, or both, set up a fund, and out of the interest of the fund, continue with their activities. After some time, such NGOs, become independent of their original sponsor and are able to work independently. A NGO should always endeavour to get a reputation of being an independent and transparent organization, to retain creditability.

Such independent NGOs, are also respected by democratic governments who would like them to study, and report without bias on the impact of government programmes and policies. Recently the Government of India had an independent assessment made of the National Rural Employment Guarantee Scheme and the report highlighted many of the weaknesses of the scheme. In Uttar Pradesh, the government requested an NGO of the State, consisting of very dedicated volunteers to study the implementation of the Rural Development Programmes in the villages. They were authorized by the State Government to interact with the concerned local authorities, see relevant files and papers and bring out an independent assessment of the programmes. On the basis of the report given by the NGO, it was found that there were many fictitious beneficiaries of the government programmes. Wrong selection of beneficiaries was done, teachers were not reporting to their schools for weeks, rations had not been issued from the fair price shops etc. This revealing report led to suspensions, transfers and also of rationalizing the implementation of the scheme. Though the NGO never asked for any money, there were complaints of the NGO demanding money for giving a favourable report. The government agencies also ganged up and began blaming the NGO for giving wrong reports, and the district authorities in some cases demanded reverification by a third agency. The State Government then dropped verification by the concerned NGO.

However, there are professional NGOs like INTACH (Indian National Trust for Art and Cultural Heritage) whose recommendations are well accepted and well recognized, both in government and the public. At the beginning, funds were provided by the Government of India, and the organization had the advantage of being headed by people, who were known experts in their field. It rose to be the foremost body in the field of preservation of architectural heritage as well as our national and cultural heritage. It had the fortune of being manned by professionals in the field of art heritage, national heritage and heritage education. They gave their lives to this organization and spread the heritage movement throughout the country. Today it is supported by dedicated heritage lovers in more than 150 cities throughout India. The NGO is consulted by the Government of India as well as the State Governments and also has Consultative status with UNO. It receives grant from the Government of India for specific project related schemes. It has retained its image as an independent entity.

But there are hundreds of NGOs working in different fields. Government has also set up an organization called CAPART to aid and assist them. The private sector has moved in very reluctantly to support or sponsor NGOs. That is why most of them seek government assistance, and hardly remain non-governmental organizations, except in name. If the NGOs were able to work independently they would represent civil society and be part of the awakening of the civil society power that is absolutely necessary today. They could also harness the energy of the unemployed youth, who otherwise pose a problem to society. They could then work extensively in the rural areas and help in empowering the people.

One area, where NGOs could extensively work, is making people aware of their rights. Today, the exploitation of the poor and the uneducated, is also because they are not aware of their rights, under the Constitution or as well as under the specific laws of the land. For instance, they are not aware of the fact that if the police arrest them, they have to be produced in court within 24 hours. If they are whisked away by the law enforcing authorities, their family members are not aware, that under the Right to Information Act, the authorities can be asked to disclose their whereabouts, within 48 hour. How many of the beneficiaries of various government programmes are even aware of the details of the scheme under which they are getting government benefits? This is particularly noticeable in schemes, involving widow pension, old age pension, scholarships for girls education, provision of housing for the poor etc. The local government official, who is aware of the ins and outs of the scheme, keeps on harassing the people (who do not monetarily satisfy him), with clauses of the scheme to enable him to deny the benefits to the individual. A government servant executing such scheme almost feels like a king, doling out money to the people, who please him. It is as if he is distributing largesse. If NGOs could take up the task of making the beneficiaries aware of these schemes, it would help not only the beneficiaries, but the government, whose image gets tarnished by faulty execution of programmes.

The Ideal Civil Servant

What has intrigued me always is that there is no unanimity in the definition of an ideal civil servant. The word 'ideal' comes from the word 'idea'. When a carpenter is making a table, there is an idea of a table in his mind. A table must have a flat surface and four legs to stand on. From this idea he is motivated to make the ideal table. The idea is the ideal concept and he tries to make his table in accordance with that idea.

What is then the idea of an ideal civil servant?. The tragedy is that no such idea of an ideal civil servant exists. This is the reason why the training in the Lal Bahadur Shastri National Academy of Administration, Mussoorie or selections by the UPSC are defective.

Should an ideal civil servant be a person who works strictly according to rules and regulations? Should an ideal civil servant strictly implement government schemes even if they are leading to harassment of the weaker sections of society? Should a civil servant mix with the public? Should a civil servant voice his opinion on policies of the government, which he is not in agreement with? Should a civil servant be strict in his behaviour or have a friendly attitude with the citizens? These, and several other questions arise in the minds of the civil servants, when they join the service. In the absence of any set guidelines on these issues, and lack of institutionalized mentoring, the civil servant meanders through life, hoping for the best.

What is the essential characteristic of the civil servant belonging to the Indian Administrative Service which distinguishes him from others? What is the 'Dharma' of such a civil servant. 'Dharma' in the *Bhagavad Gita* implies the essential nature of anything, without which it cannot retain its independent existence. For example, heat and light are the 'Dharma' of the Sun. We cannot conceive of a cold Sun or a Dark Sun.

What then is the essential nature or the 'Dharma' of the IAS?

I feel that the following definition is worth considering.

The Dharma of a civil servant is the impartial and humane implementation of public policies, within the confines of the Constitution and within the mandate of law.

Let us analyse each characteristic of the above definition.

Impartial	:	Implies, without any discrimination of caste, creed, sex, religion and political views.
Just	:	Implies, not only in accordance with law, but in accordance with natural justice, keeping in view the dignity of the individual.
Public Policies	:	Implies the policies laid down by the elected government of the day.
Constitution	:	Implies the national consensus on the principles on the basis of which the State has to run.

This definition of the Dharma of the civil servant has to be universally acceptable by the government as well the citizens, including the people's representatives. Not doing so will lead to friction between the stakeholders in governance.

A civil servant often finds himself in a quandary. If he acts strictly according to his dharma and points out the rules and regulations in any particular matter, the politician, who is supporting the case, tends to view the noting of the civil servant as obstructionist. The political master also often tells the civil servant that if everybody was to merely follow these rules and regulations, then why should they come to him (the minister), and therefore the civil servant must advise him instead on the methods by which the particular request can be accepted.

It once happened, when Vishwanath Pratap Singh was the Chief Minister of Uttar Pradesh, that numerous requests for installing state tube wells were coming. Each MLA was pressing for the tube well to be installed in his constituency. Sri VP Singh asked me to prepare criteria on the basis of which State tube wells should be sanctioned. I prepared about ten points like groundwater level, distance from the nearest state tube well, the habitations and fields which would be served by the tube well, etc. Sri VP Singh gave his approval to the criterion with some amendments and we began to sanction tube wells according to the approved criterion. After two weeks the MLAs came to see him complaining that if the tube wells were to be only sanctioned according to the fixed criteria, what would be the value of their recommendations. Sri VP Singh had no answer. Politics has its own standards!

By the very nature of civil society in developing economies, the civil servant is a part of a well educated elite, well read and well informed on global issues. On the other hand, the majority of the remaining population, suffer from illiteracy or low levels of education, and therefore, civil servants in such emerging economies also become leaders of change.

Even the ministers might not be so well educated. In such a situation, the Dharma of a civil servant would be not only the sincere implementation of policies, but also formulation of the policies. His Dharma would also include educating his political master and making him familiar on international issues. He should suggest solutions, based on how the same situation in other countries, which have already experienced this problem, were solved.

It is also the Dharma of the civil servant to ensure the best results for the money spent by the government. By definition, developing economies do not have adequate resources of their own and can therefore ill afford wasteful expenditure. The civil servant must, therefore, dissuade the political masters from being populist and from adopting short term solutions, and persuade him to concentrate on long term planning.

The Dharma of a civil servant should also be to be innovative so that he does not administer with a closed mind. He should have a positive approach, where all new ideas should be welcomed and 'no' would be the last word. He must administer with compassion and sympathy because he is only an arbitrator in conflicting claims amongst equals. His is the power of arbitration, as a representative of the government, which has been elected by the people.

Chapter 11

The Evening Years

On September 15th, 2007, I demitted the office of Secretary-General Rajya Sabha. A resolution was adopted by the entire Rajya Sabha, commending my services to the House. The Chairman, Sri Hamid Ansari, read out the resolution and it was adopted by acclamation. I rose up from my chair, bowed to all the members with folded hands, and sat down. There is no practice of the outgoing Secretary-General speaking in the House or giving a farewell speech.

As I moved back to my room, after the singing of the Vande Mataram, several members came to see me and thanked me for all the cooperation given to them. All my personal staff, and the senior officials of the Rajya Sabha secretariat shook hands. I was then escorted to my car.

As I moved back to my house, with several officials in cars, following me, I had a sense of satisfaction. I had done my job to the best of my abilities, and earned the love and respect of the members as well as my staff. What more could I have wanted.

After some days, Sri Anil Ambani of the Reliance Anil Dhirubhai Ambani Group telephoned me and requested me to join as an Independent Director on the Board of Reliance Power. I had first met Anil Ambani with his father, when I was Chief Secretary, Uttar Pradesh. Together with the Chief Minister we were meeting the industrialists of Mumbai, to attract investment in Uttar Pradesh. We had then been called for dinner by Sri Dhirubhai Ambani at his residence, where we met the family. Dhirubhai Ambani and both Anil and Mukesh were extremely forward-looking individuals and I had been deeply impressed by their new initiatives in the IT and mobile sectors. I had subsequently met Anil Ambani in the Rajya Sabha when he was nominated as a member by the President of India. He had subsequently resigned but our friendship remained.

It was kind of him to have offered the Directorship and I immediately accepted.

In December 2007, the Government of India was setting up the New Pension Scheme (NPS). This covered all the government servants of the Central Government who had joined after 1st January 2004. I was offered the post of Chairman of the New Pension Scheme Trust, which I accepted. This required the chairing of meetings of the Trust every quarter. The government had decided to move over to the contributory pension scheme where the civil servant was required to contribute 10% of his pay and together with equal contribution from the government, the entire amount was sent to the Trust for putting it in the market, in shares and bonds. Fund managers were appointed by the Trust, and their performance was judged based on the returns they generated.

Sri Prabhat Kumar, our former Cabinet Secretary, and an icon from the University days, invited me to join the IC Centre for Governance. It was very satisfying to discuss issues relating to governance. We used to also go to Panchgani for lectures and discussions.

I had been elected as the President of the Alumni Association of the Indian Institute of Public Administration. I now got more time to activate it. I had earlier served as the Vice-President of the IIPA. To increase the resources of the IIPA, I organized a new programme involving training of Public Sector executives in Leadership. The IIPA faculty of Ms Roma and Taneja carried out the training very enthusiastically.

In 2008, SK Misra, Chairman of Indian National Trust for Art and Cultural Heritage, met me at the annual get together of the Muirians (Hostel of Allahabad University) and invited me to join as Member Secretary of the organization. It was a full time job and as it related to my first love, of art and culture, I readily agreed. It was a wonderful experience to work with a dynamic officer like SK Misra, who had become famous for his work in the field of tourism in Haryana. After working for two years in INTACH both of us moved out and in 2012 started another heritage conservation organization called the Indian Trust for Rural Heritage and Development (ITRHD). We have now undertaken (a) conservation work in Maluti, Jharkhand, where we are restoring the terracotta temples, (b) preserving the heritage of the three villages of Azamgarh (Hariharpur, Mubarakpur and Nizamabad) and (c) a mosque in Haryana. SK Misra is not only a devoted conservationist but a fund raiser, which talent, it is difficult to match!

I had been the President of the National Wushu Association, a martial art recognized by the Olympic Association of India as well as the Asian Games. We got this sport recognized by the Sports Ministry of the Government of India, as well as the CBSE Board, the National Police Sports Association, the CRPF and the Army. This also gave me an opportunity to visit the Beijing Olympics in 2004. It gave me immense satisfaction to see thousands of our youths practising this sport, all over India.

I wanted to do something for the city I live in – Noida. I found an individual, Trilok Sharma, who ran a communication agency, Greycell Marcom and who gave me an idea of hosting a Conclave where the senior most officials of Noida and the Government of Uttar Pradesh, could have an open dialogue on the problems facing the residents as well as the industrialists of Gautam Budh Nagar. We have been successful in organizing the NGY Conclave annually where citizens and the authorities of Noida interact with each other. This has pioneered several new initiatives in the field of health, education and sanitation in the area.

In Noida, I discovered a very active NGO called the Noida Lok Manch, which had Sri Prabhat Kumar as its President. The spirit behind the NGO was a person Mahesh Saxena, who has been running this NGO for the last two decades. This NGO manages the only cremation ground in Noida called the Antim Niwas. It also runs three schools. After joining the NGO I got them a Community Radio license and we now run the Radio Lok Manch. The NGO also manages the Noida Public Library, owned by the Noida Authority. Several eminent people like Sushil Tripathi, Justice Garg, Prashant Misra are members of this organization. It is very satisfying to work with such NGOs after retirement.

My close friends suggested that post retirement is the time when we should see the world. We formed a group called Globetrotters led by our dynamic leader, Colonel Valmiki Katju who was also from our Boys High School, Allahabad. Dear friends like Vinod Vaish, Jayant Sanyal, Rajani Kant Verma, Subhash Bose and others also joined the group. We toured Bali, Angkor Vat, Poland, Austria, Krakow, Norway, Moscow, Leningrad, Germany, St Petersburg, Greece, Turkey in successive years. It was great fun. Old age, we found, is no bar to enjoyment. The spouses also joined in these tours. I strongly feel that such trips with old friends leads to further bonding.

Being one of the few officers who had served as Secretary-General of Rajya Sabha, I found myself in an elite group called the 'experts'. The TV anchors are always looking for people who can authoritatively express themselves on issues which crop up from time to time, based on one's experience in the concerned sector. Having also served in Defence, I am also called on panels discussing defence issues. While in service one can only express the views of the government. But once we retire, we can express ourselves freely and honestly. But for this, it is also necessary to keep our knowledge up-to-date. This requires intensive studies and reading.

If you do not want the evening of life to turn to dusk speedily, be mentally and physically active. Learn to live life happily and enjoy the pleasures which your children and their children give you. That is your right which you have earned.

Index